# Fantastic Flowers

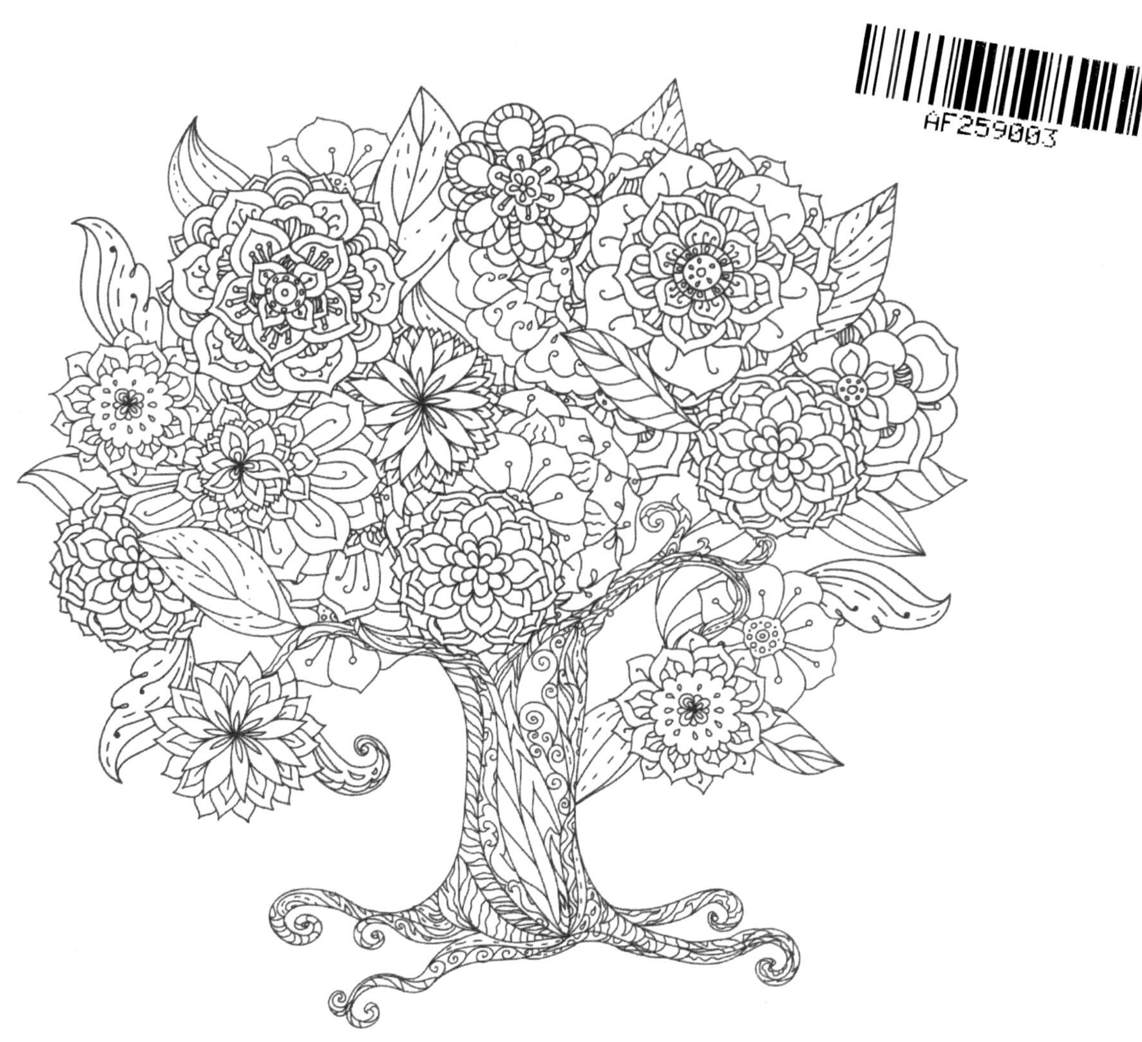

## Alex Noelle

# Fantastic Flowers

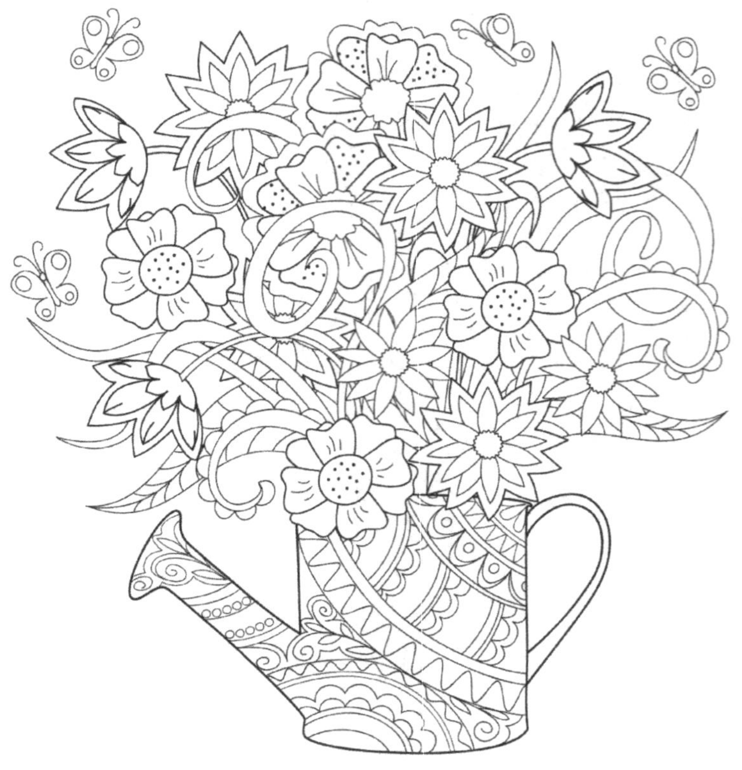

Copyright © 2021 by Alex Noelle.

No part of this book may be used or reproduced in any manner whatsoever without the prior written permission of the author.

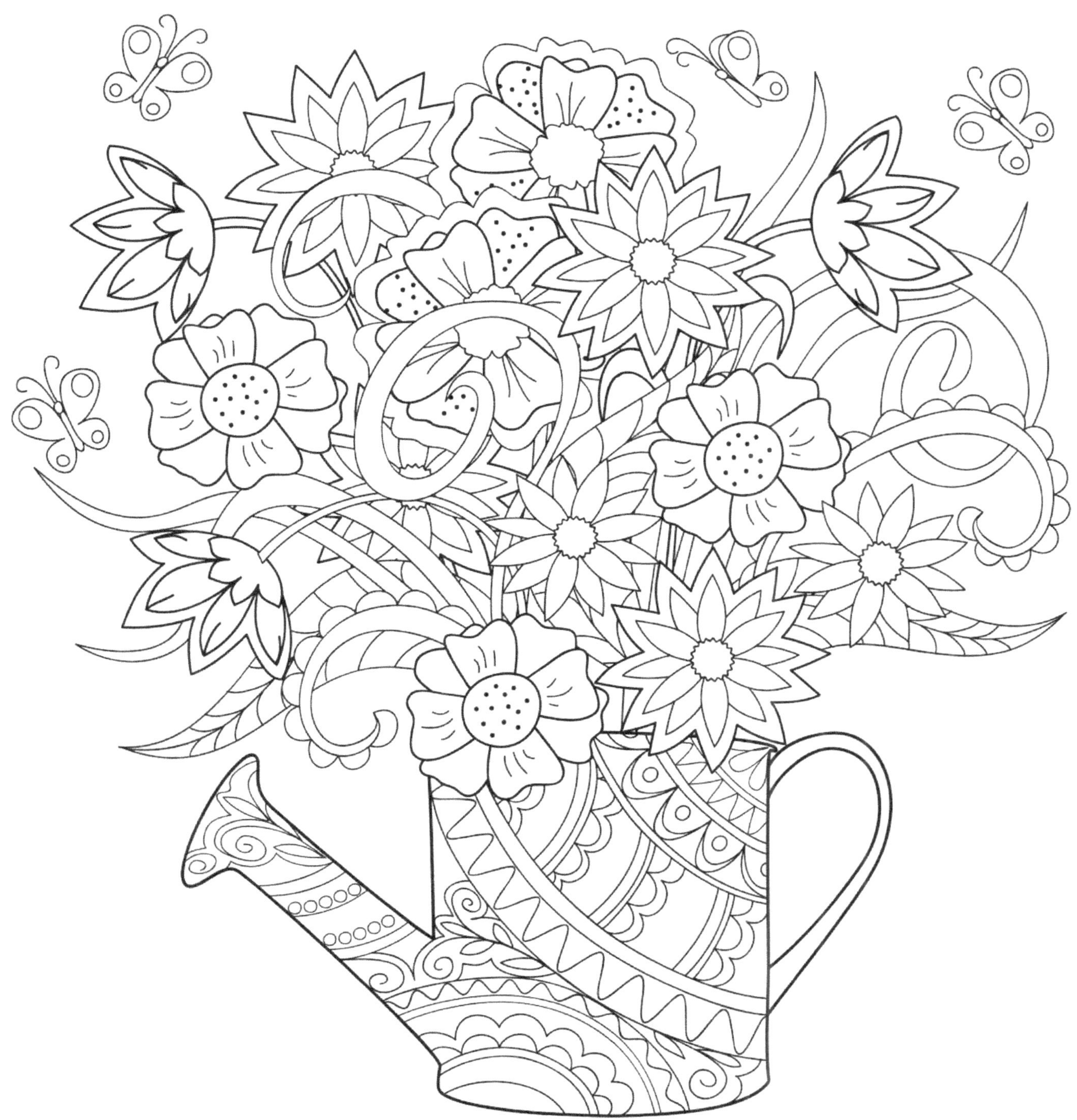

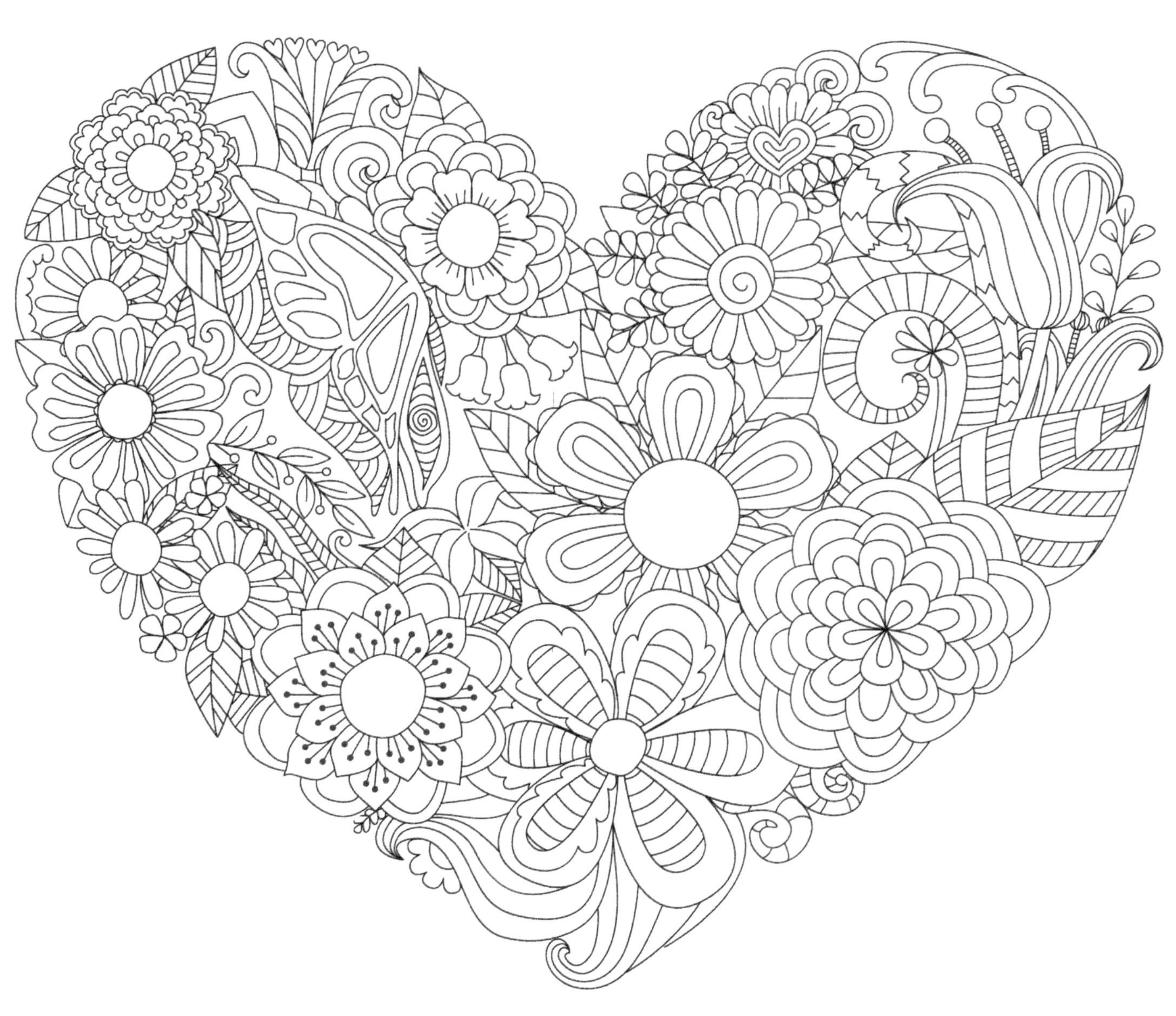

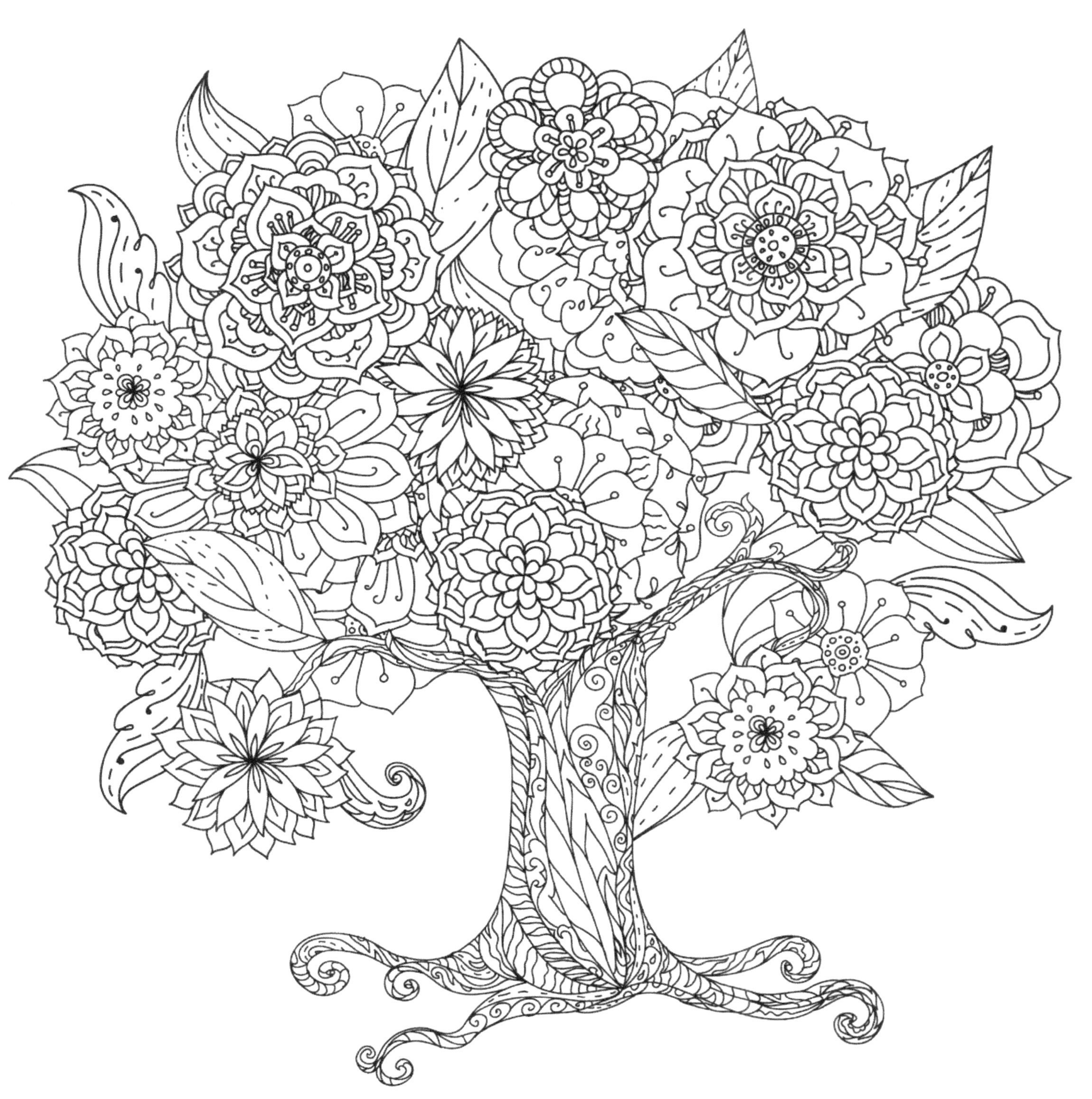

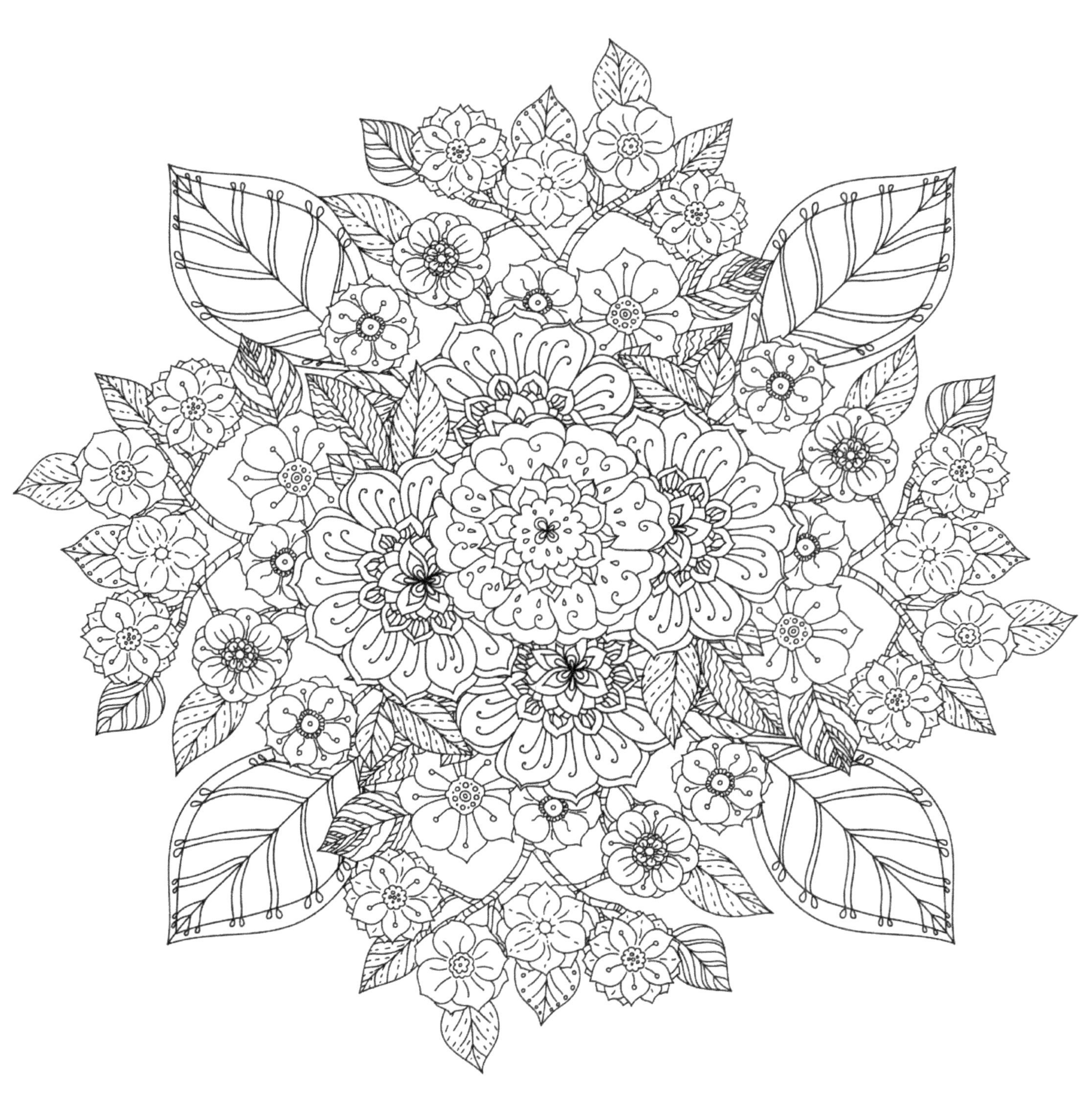

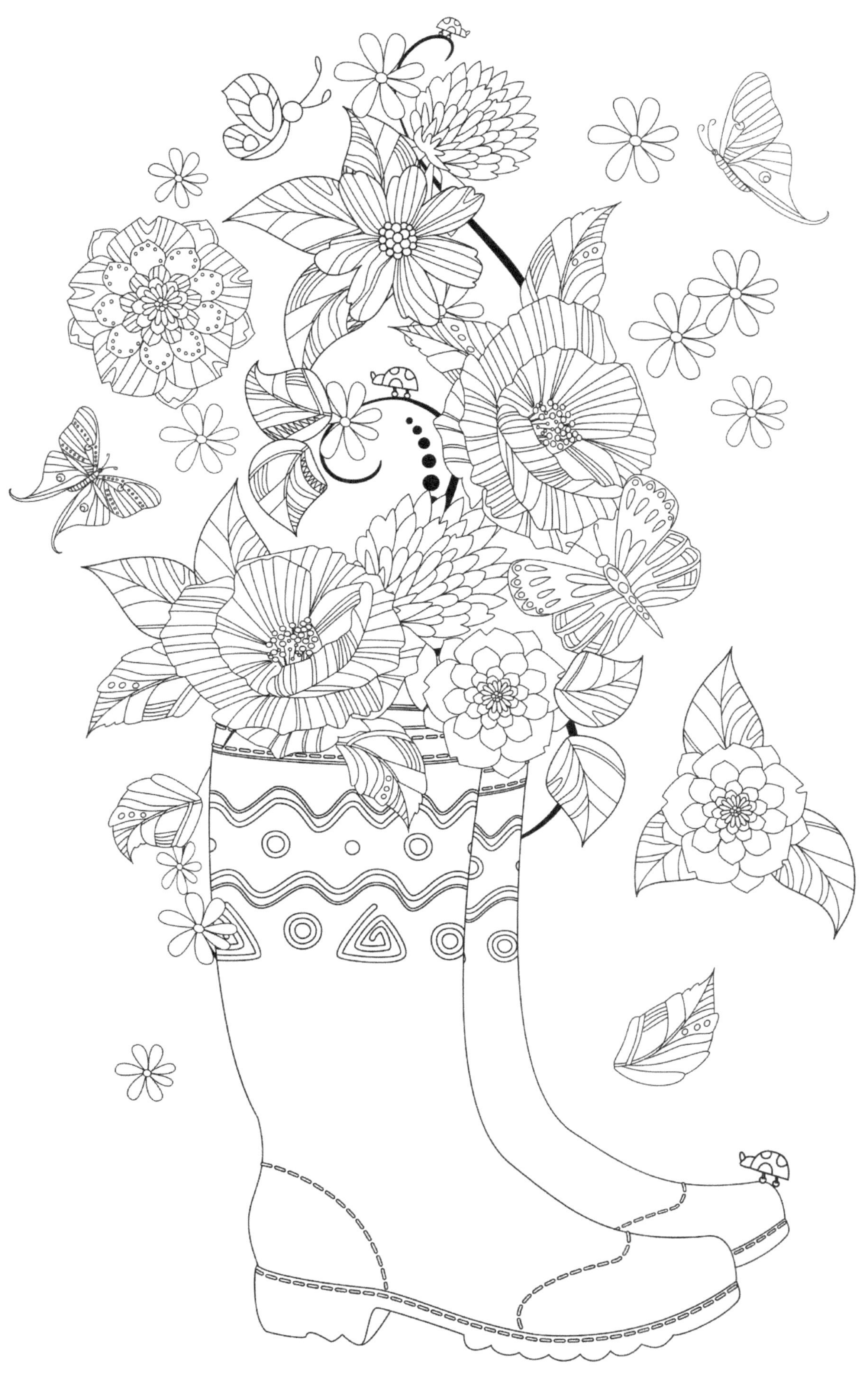

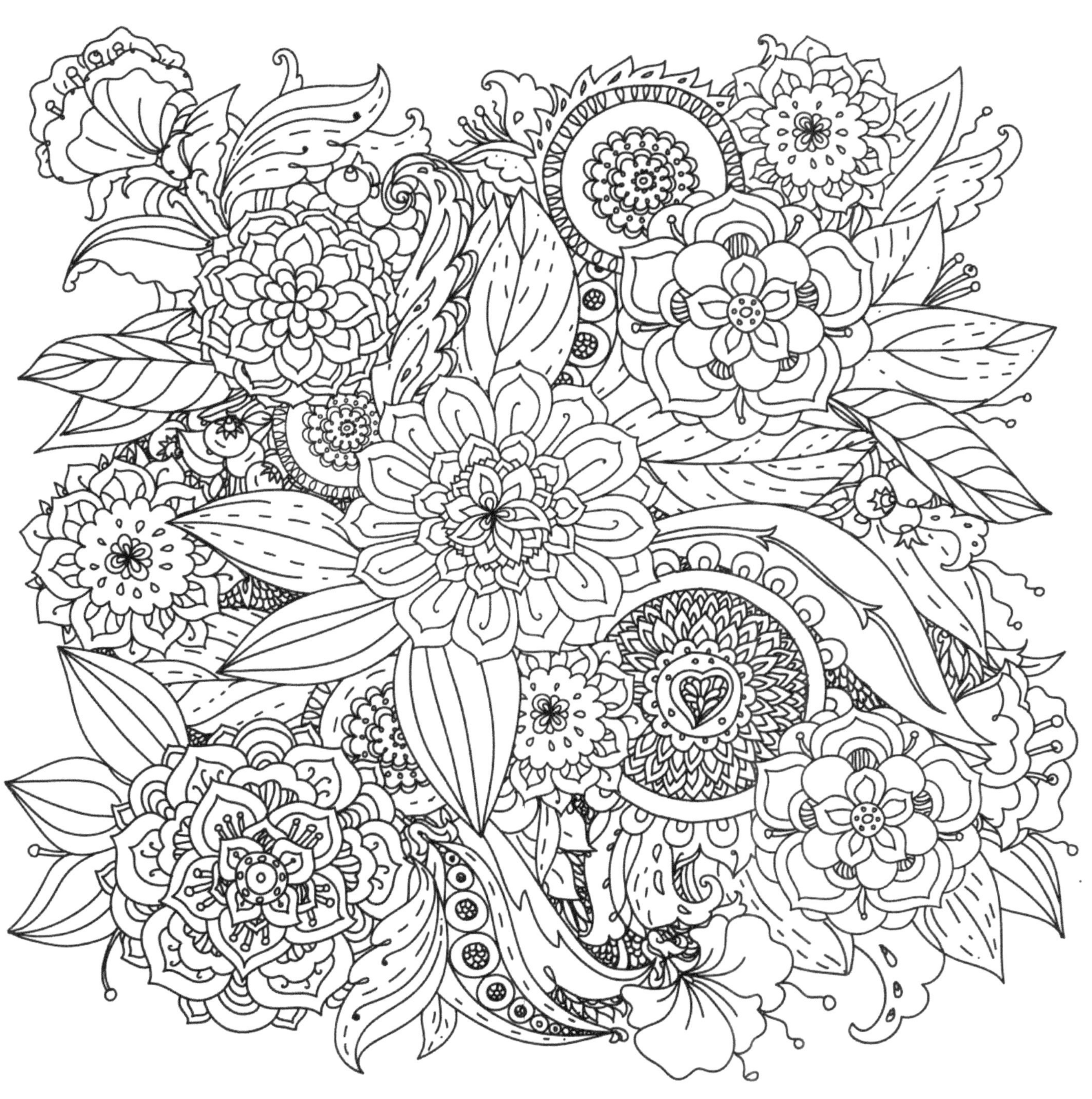

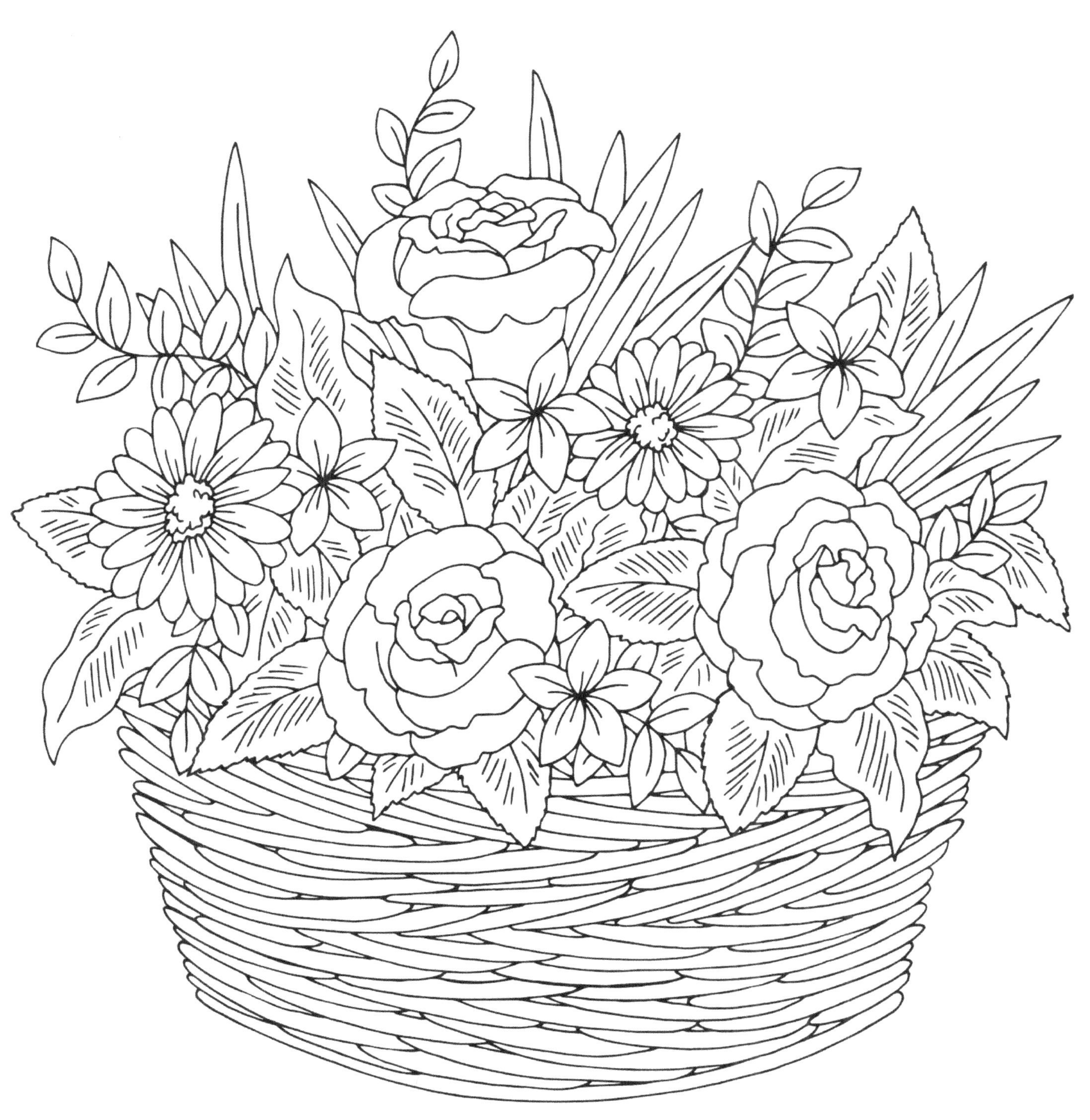

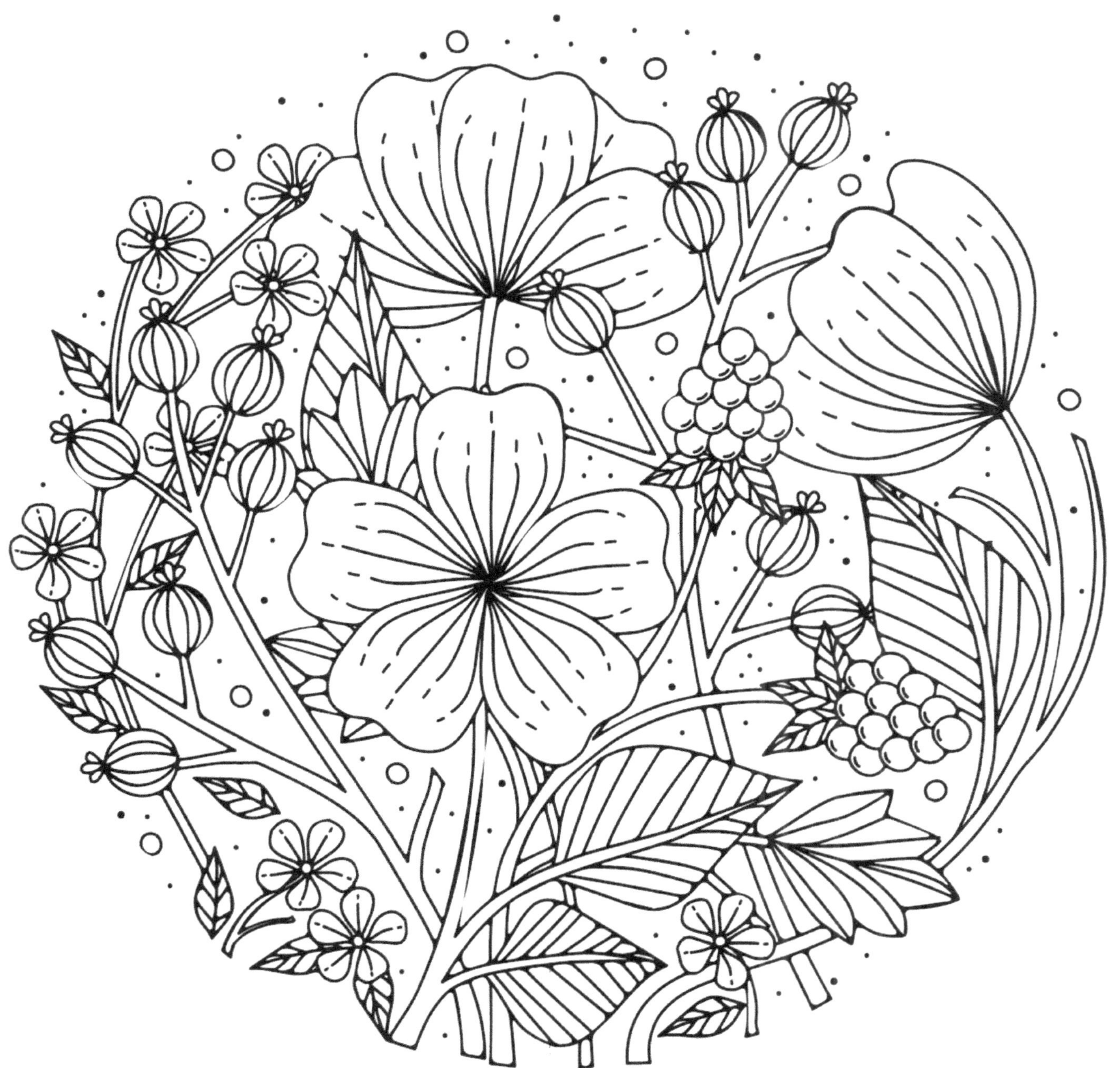

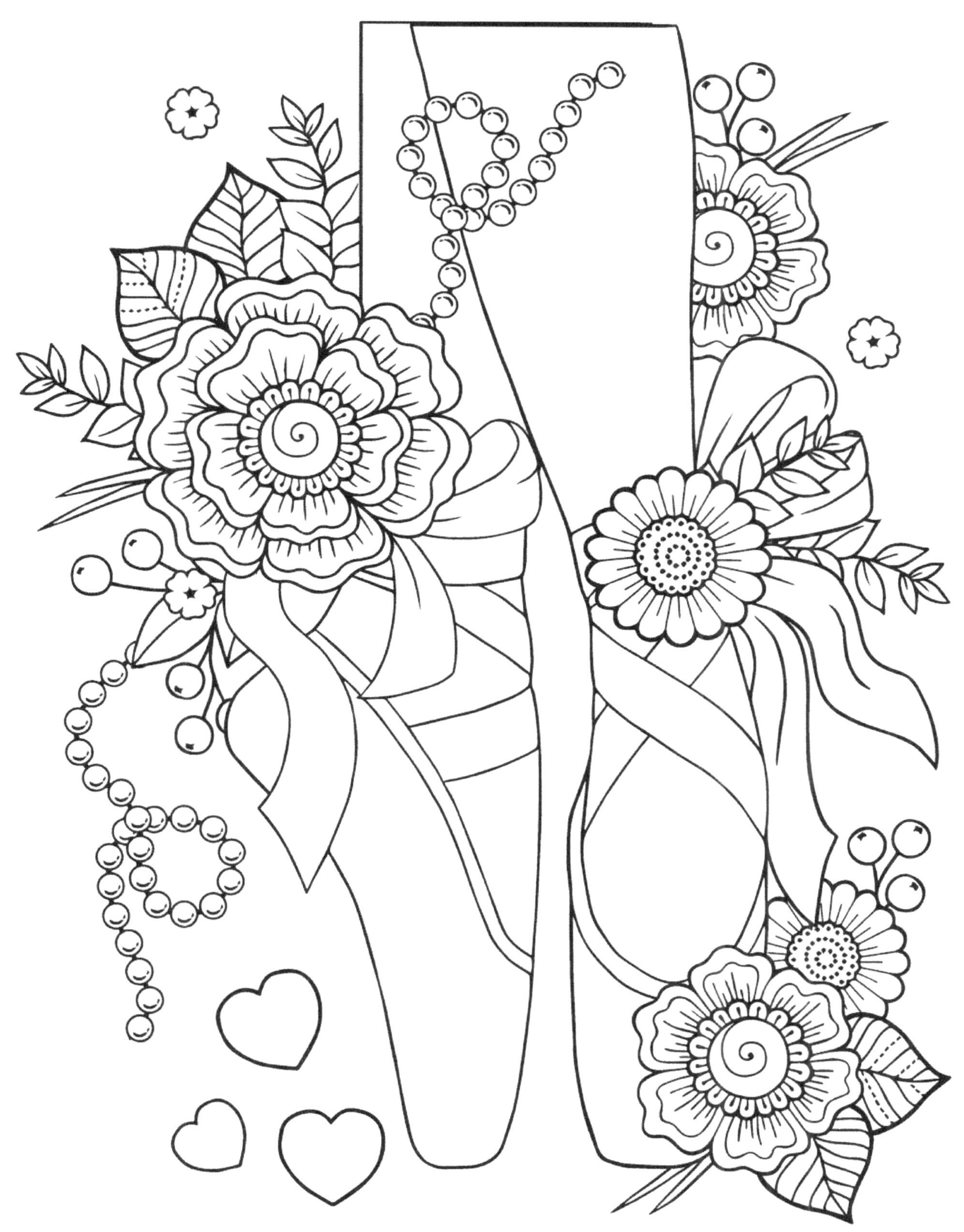

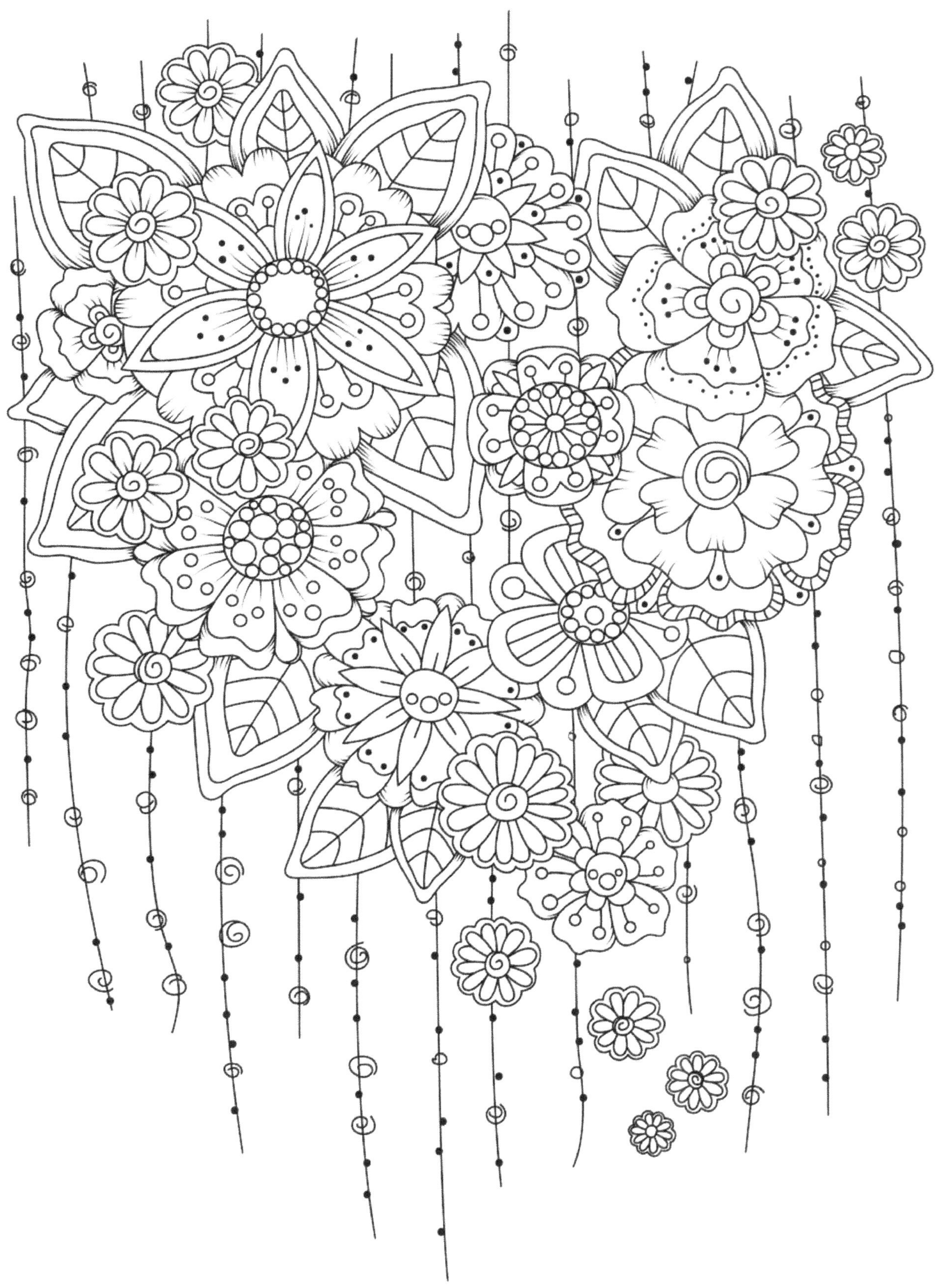

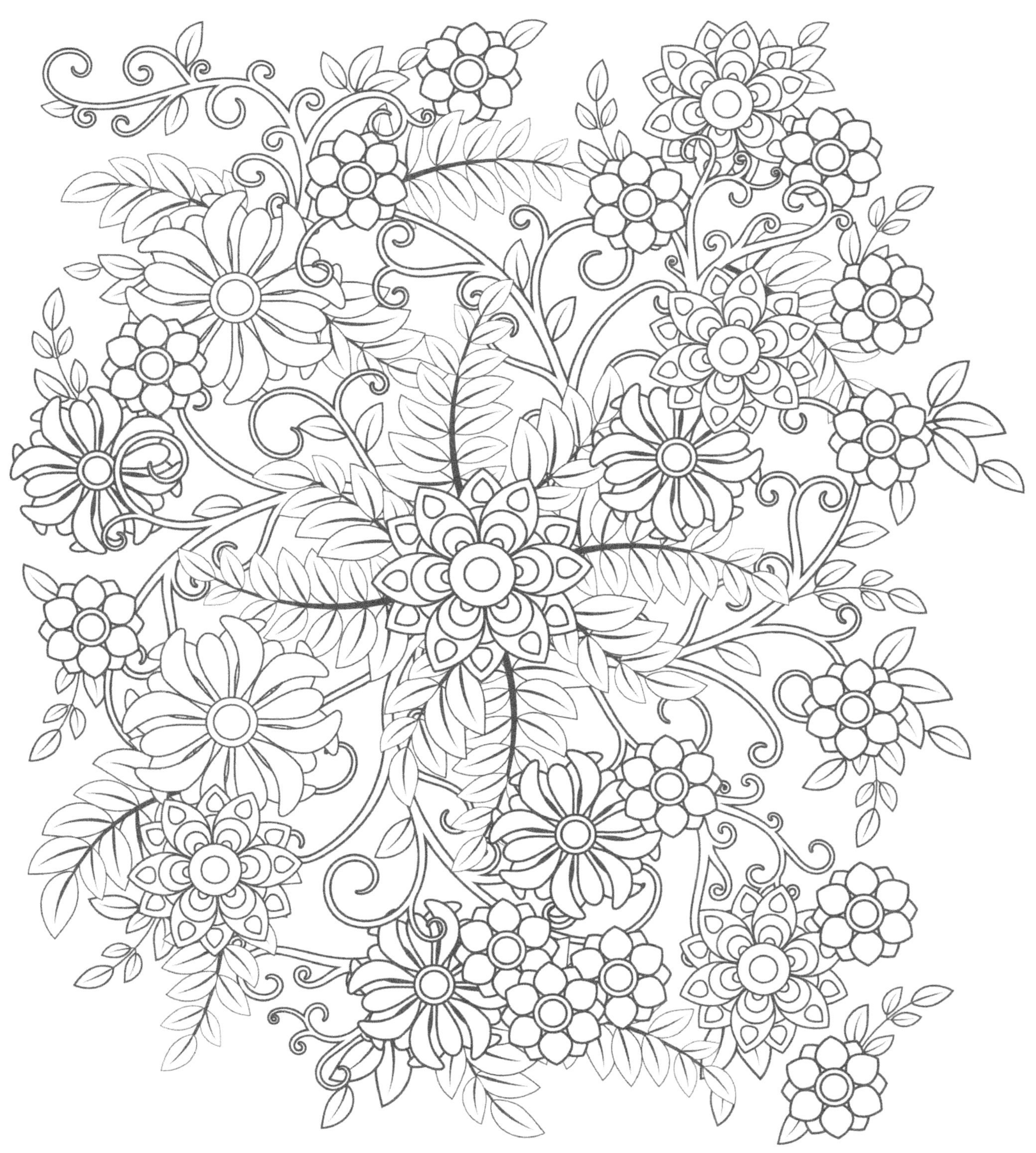

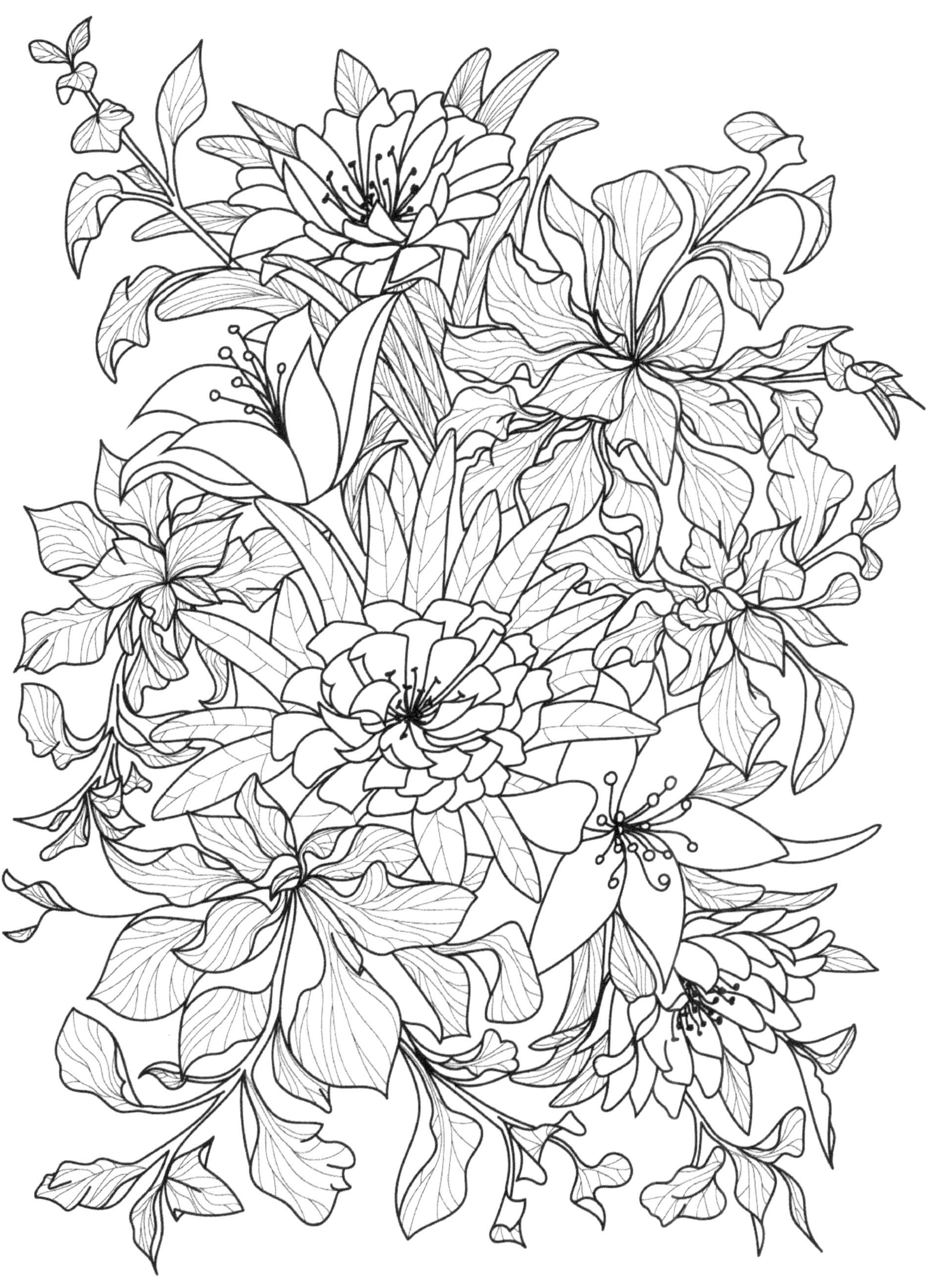

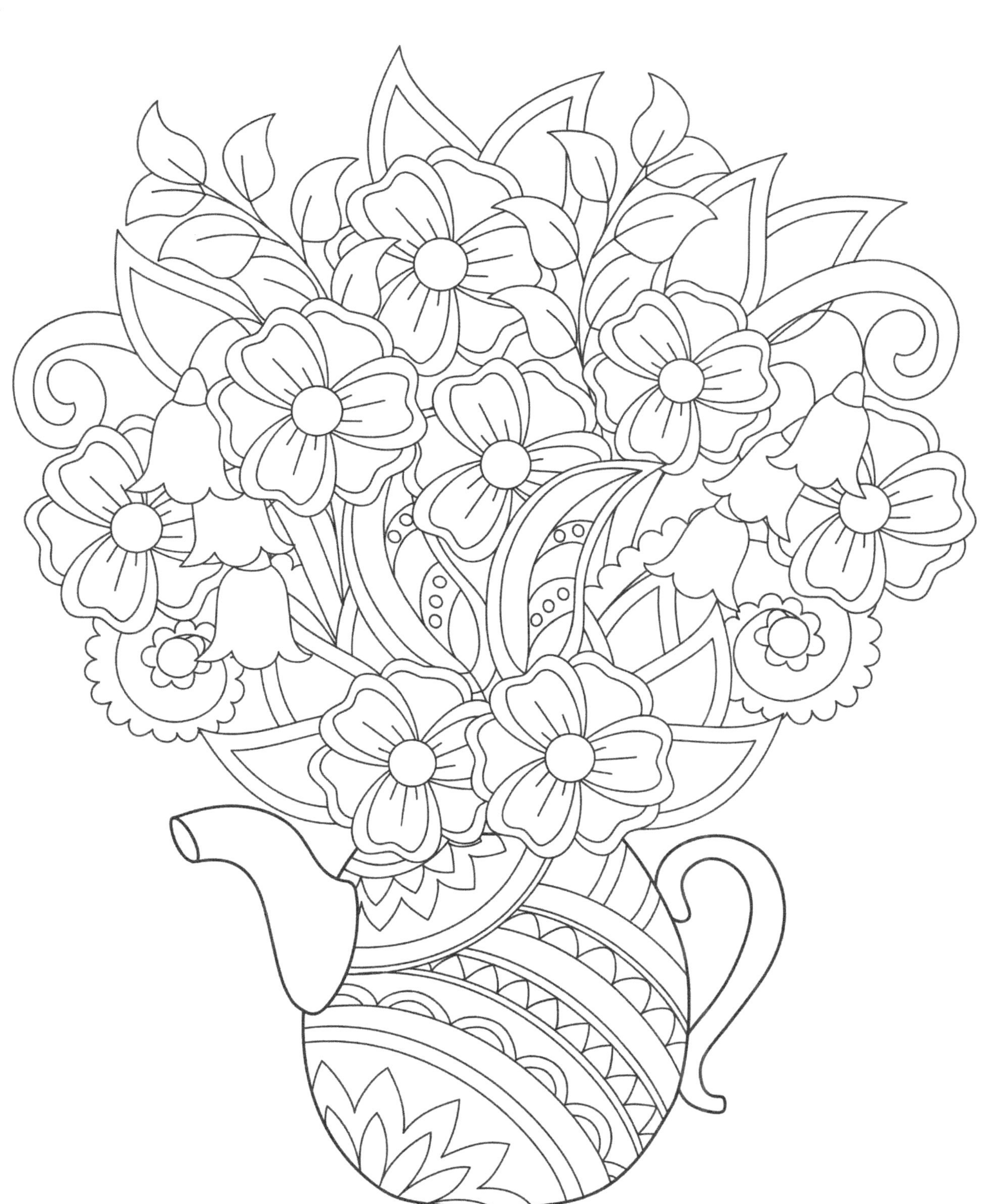

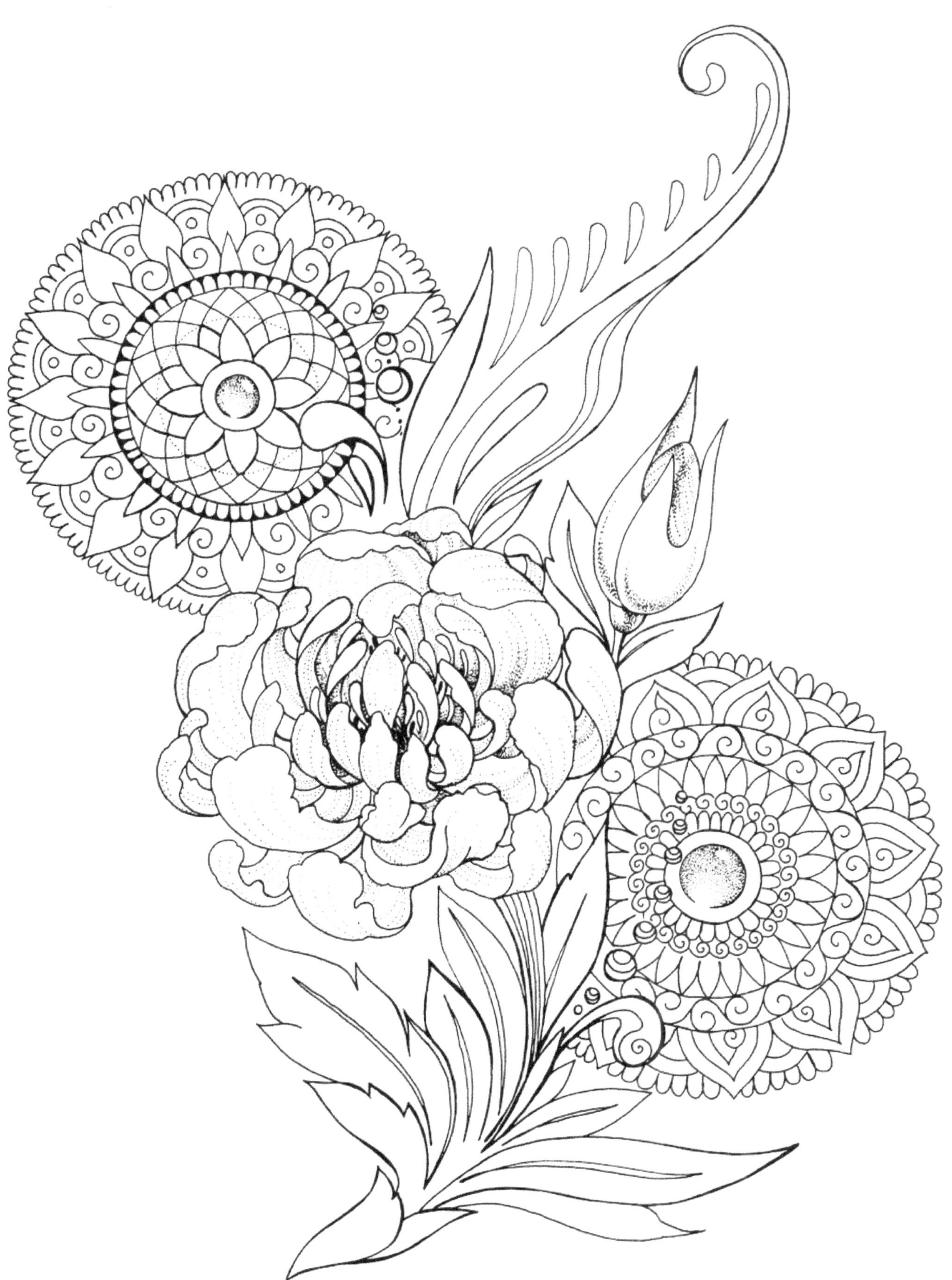

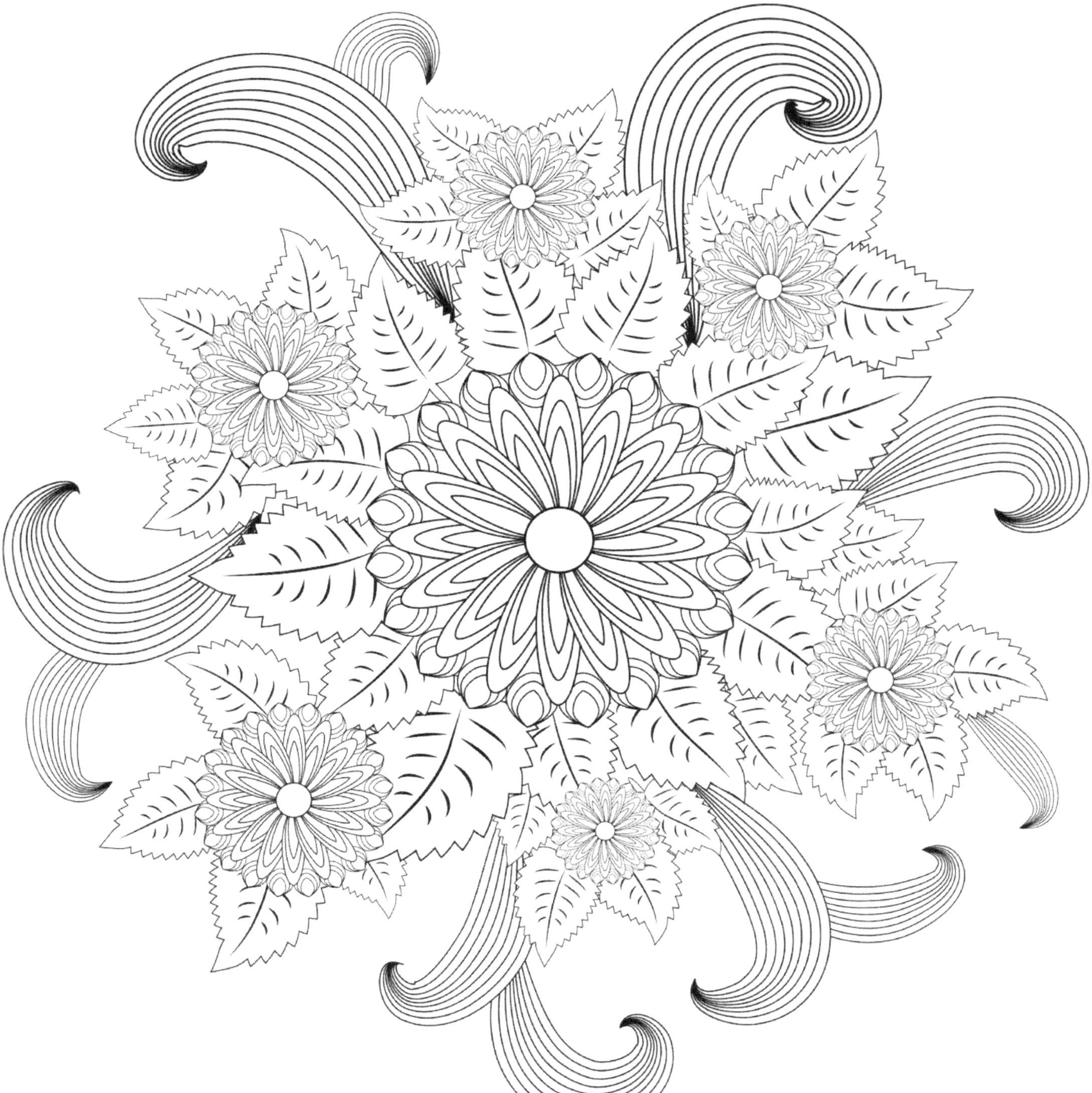

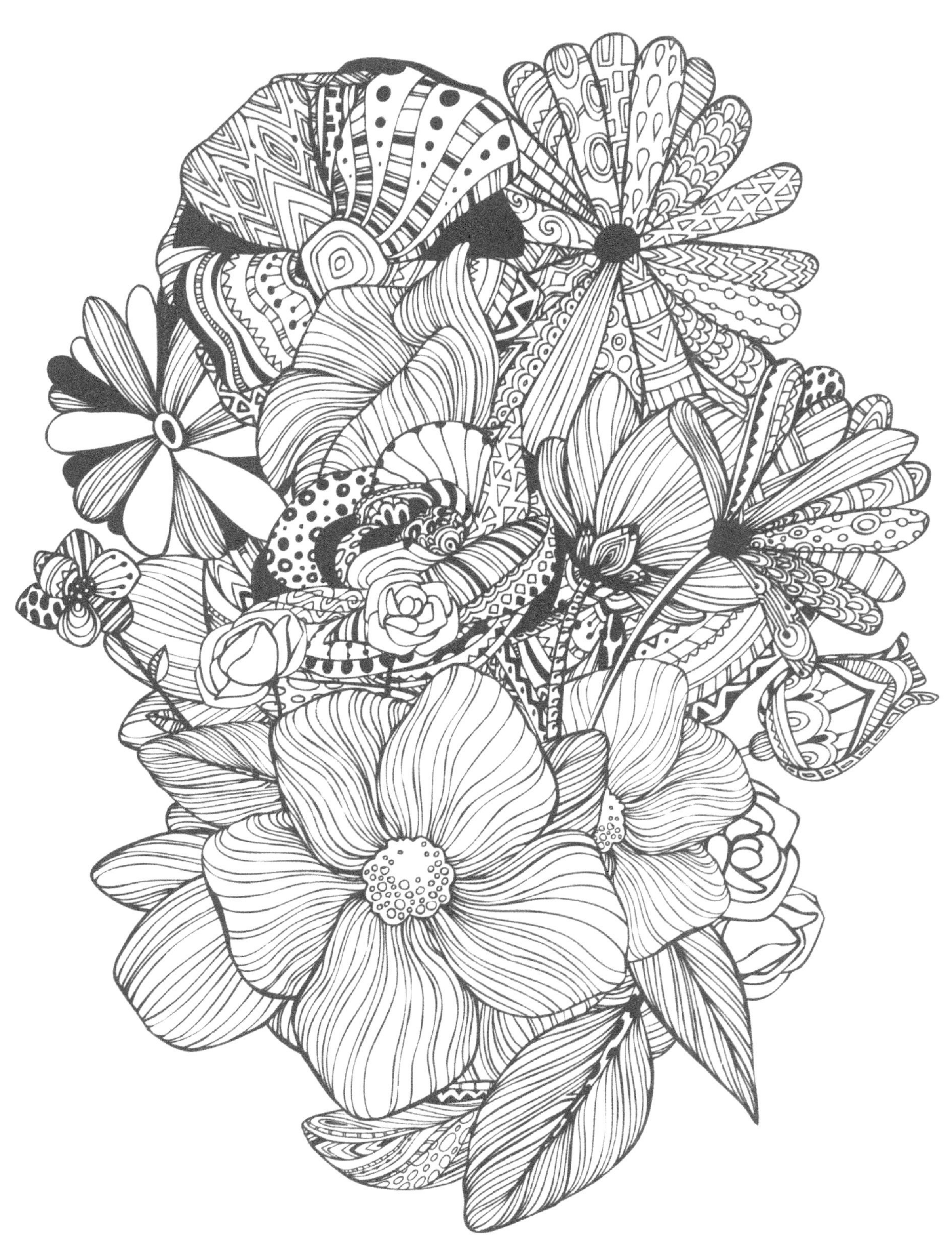

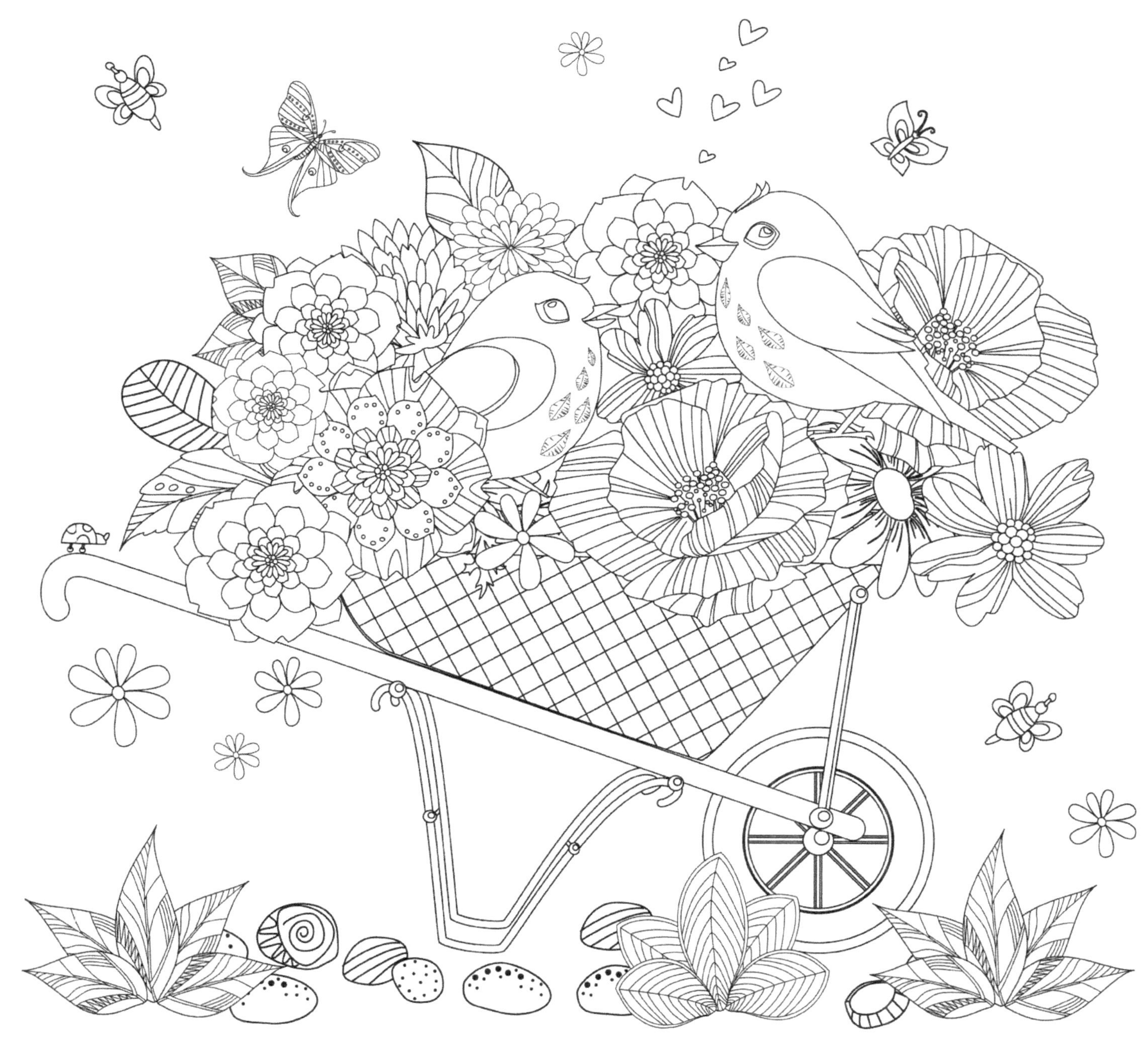

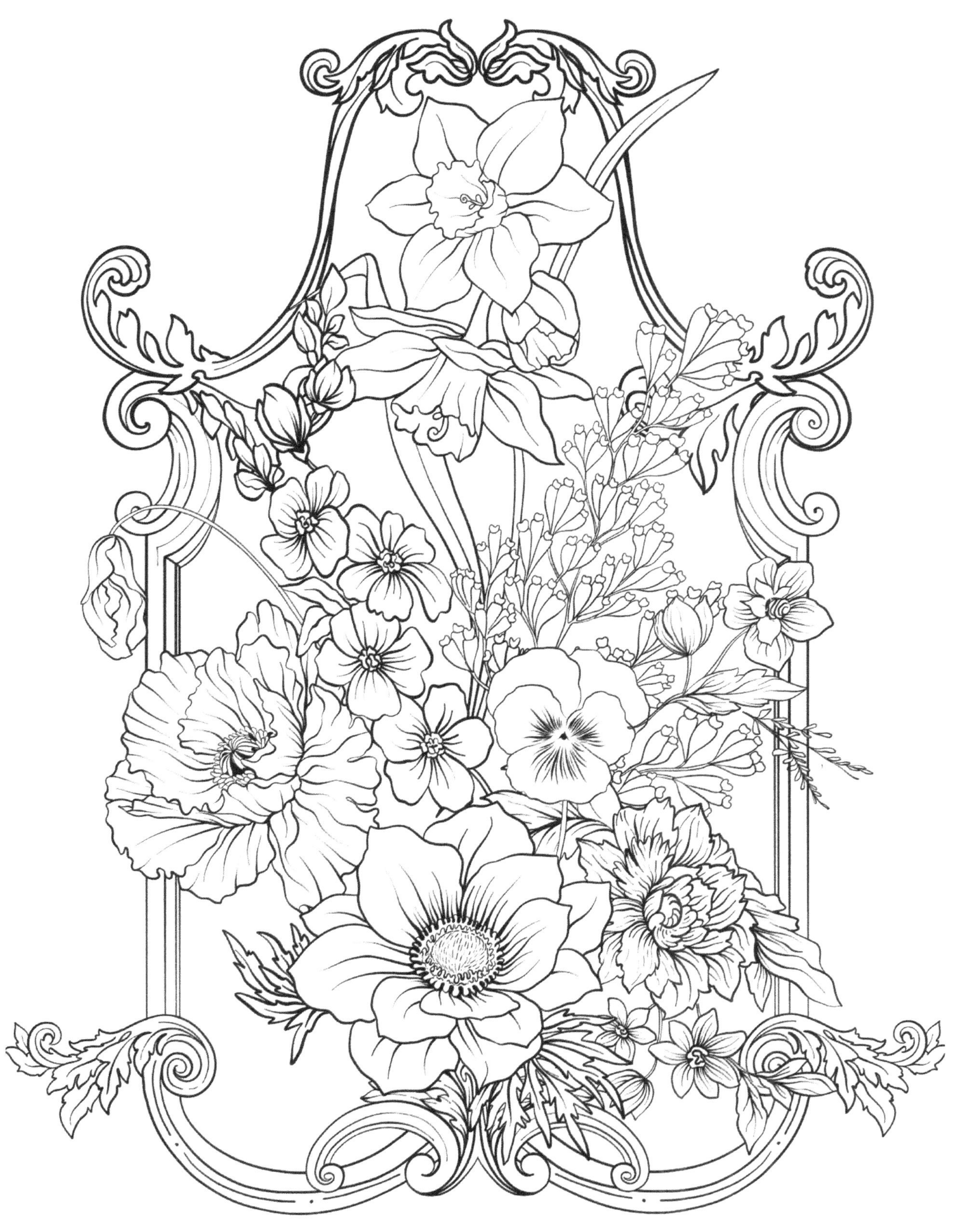

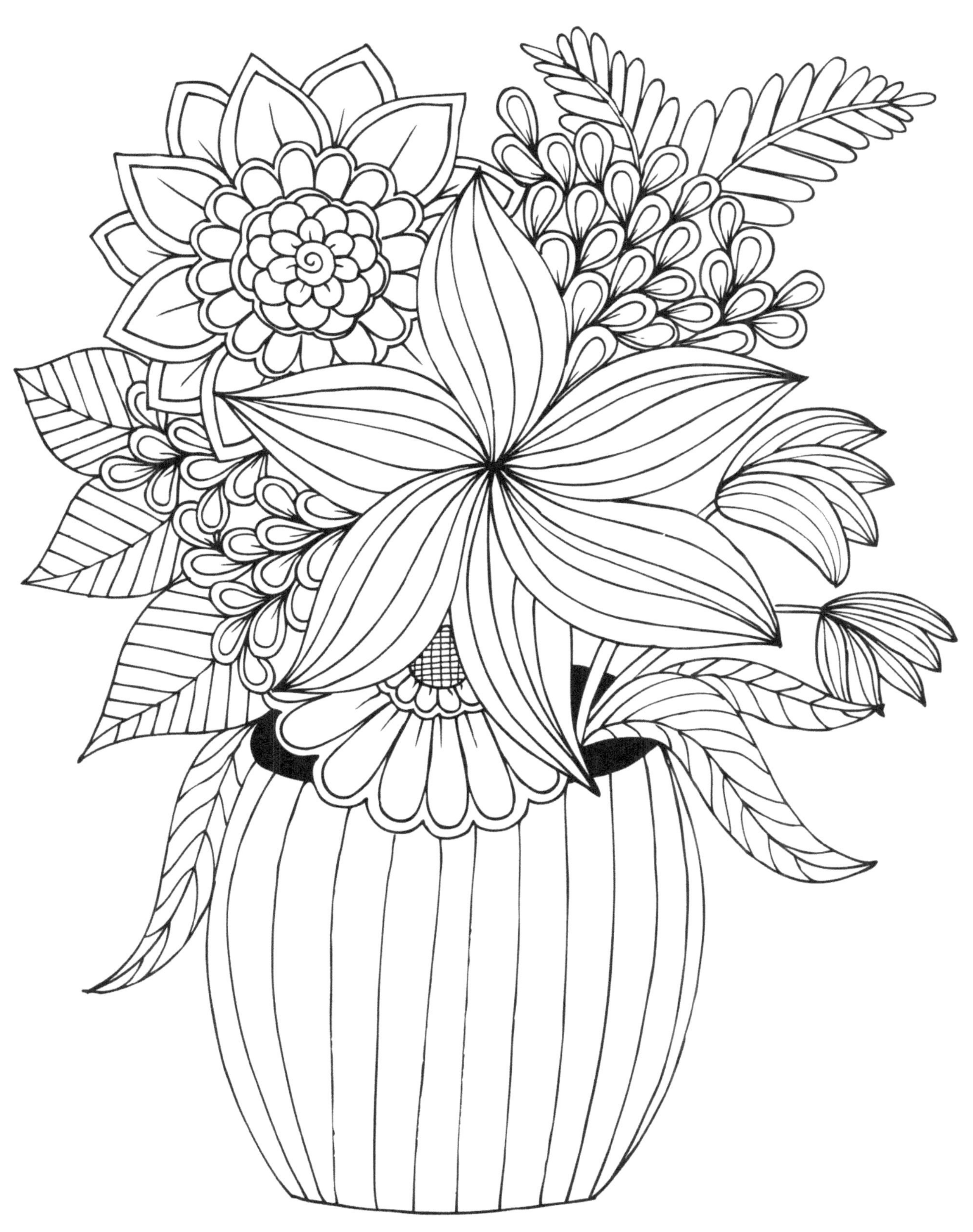

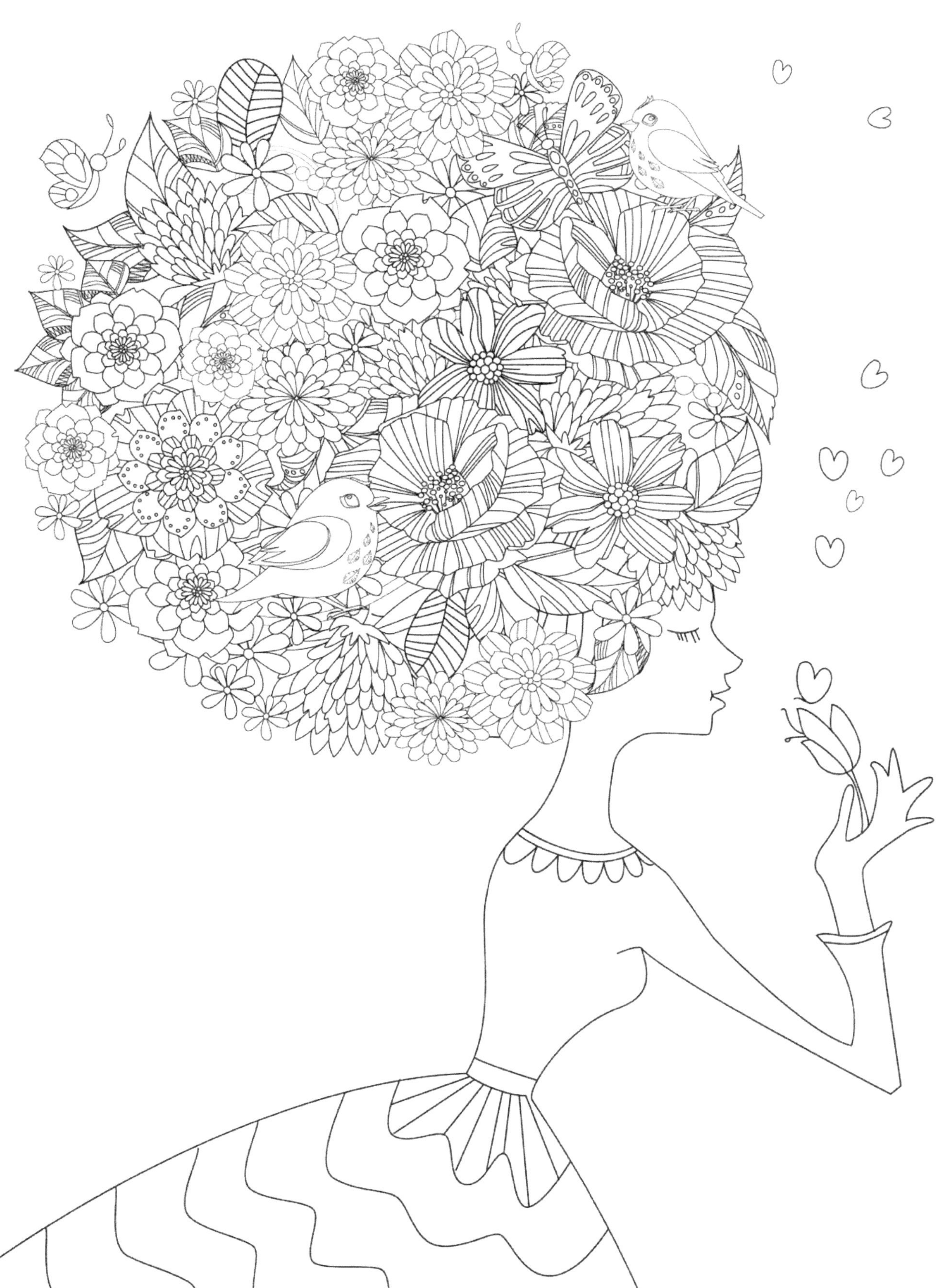

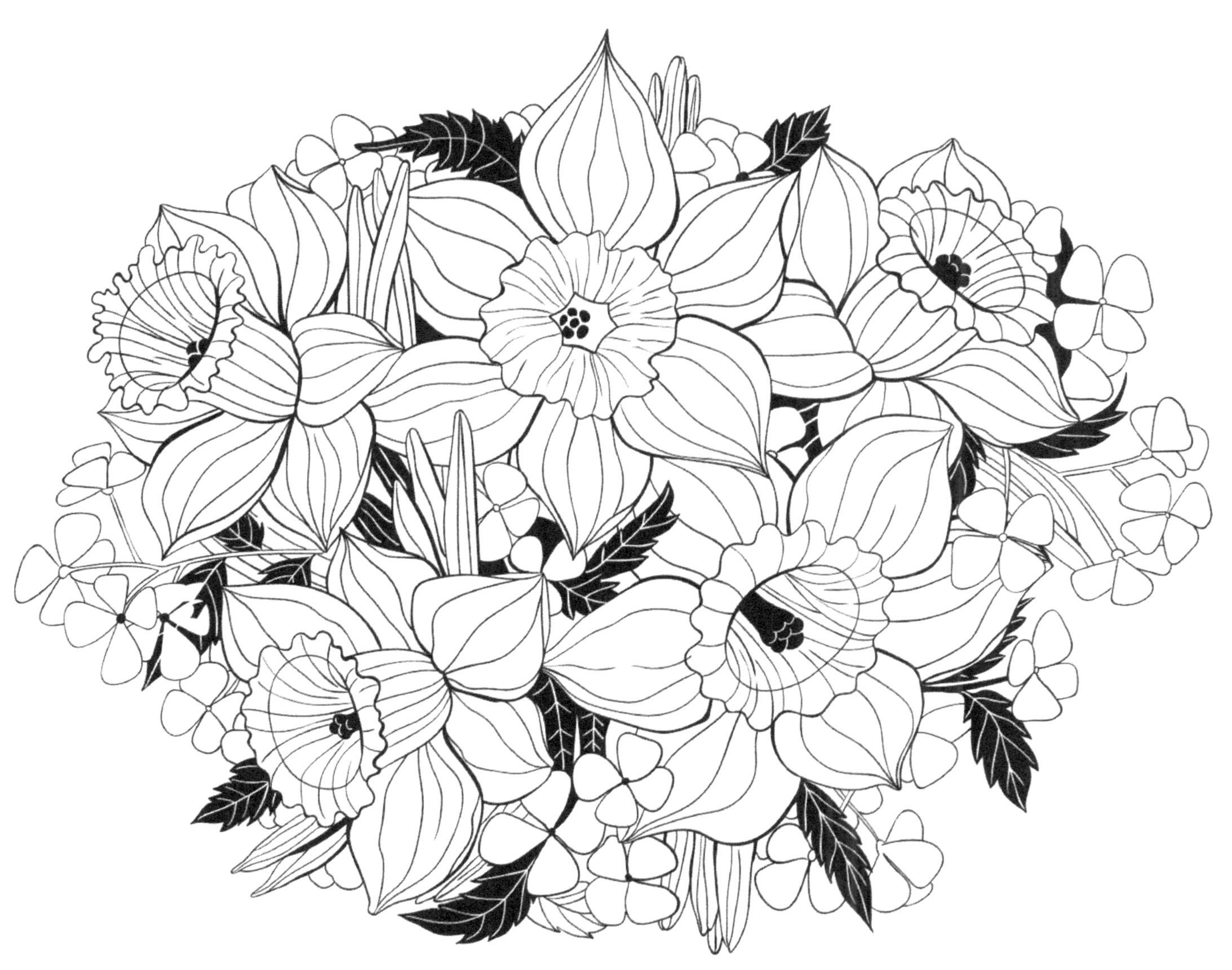

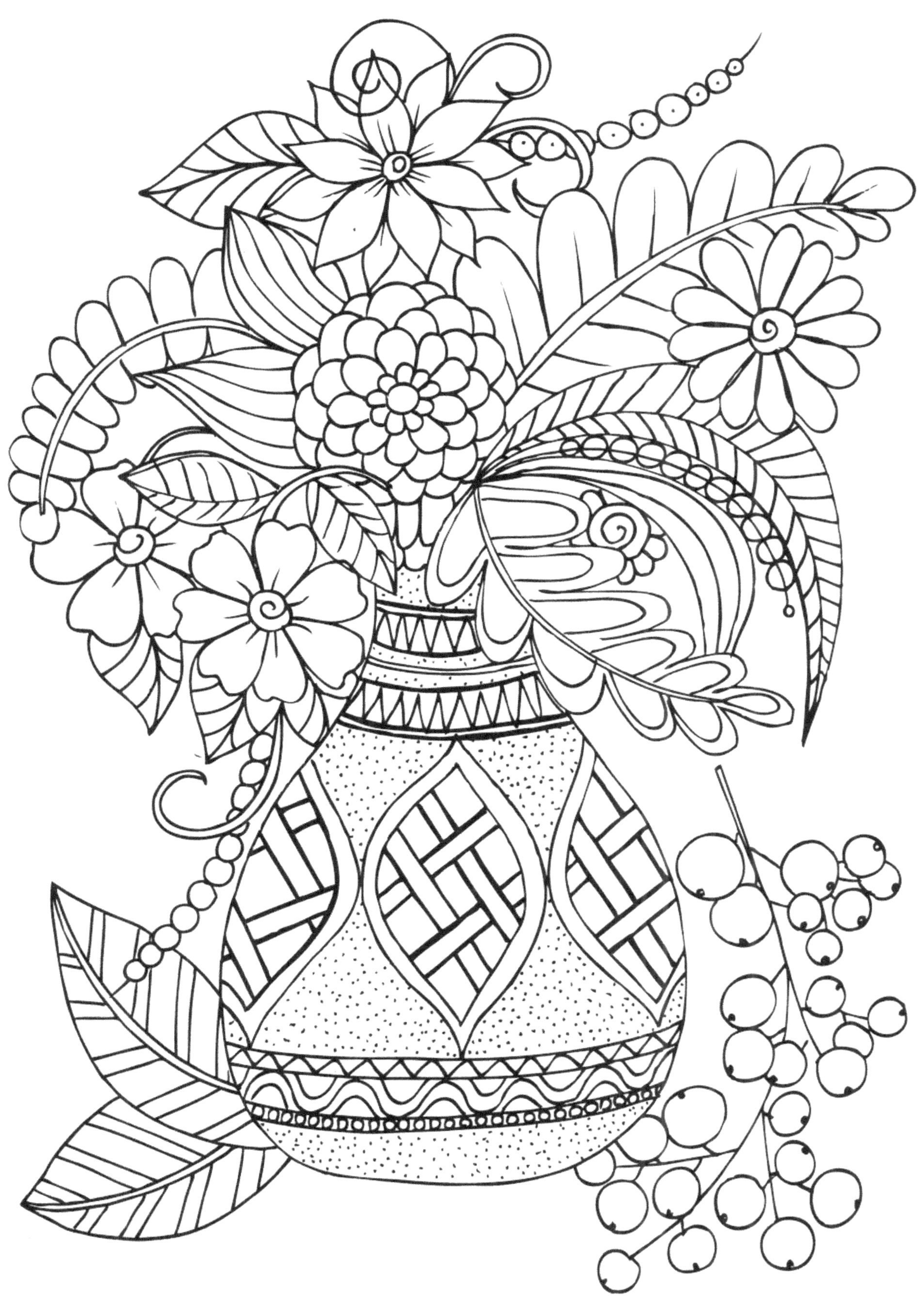

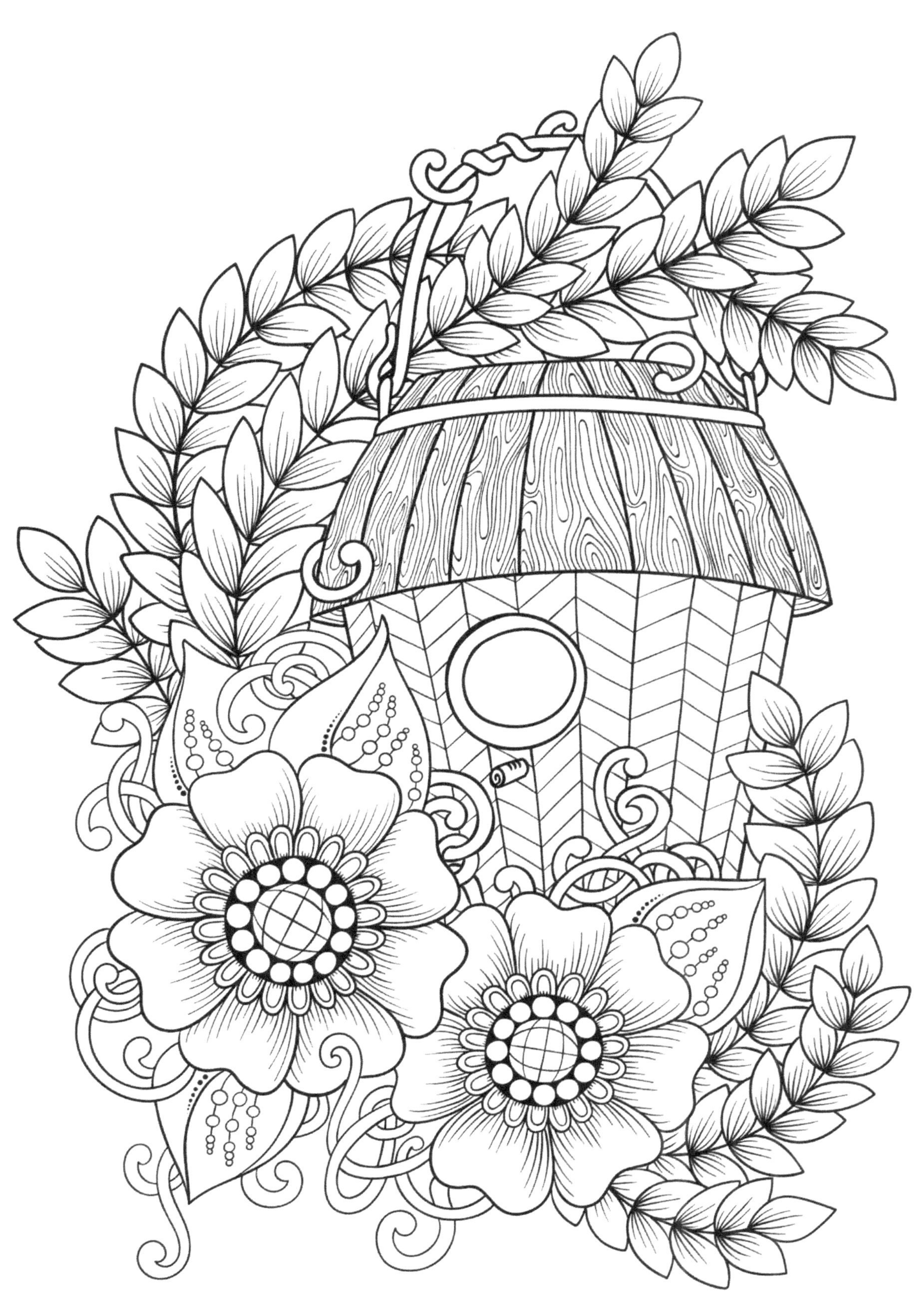

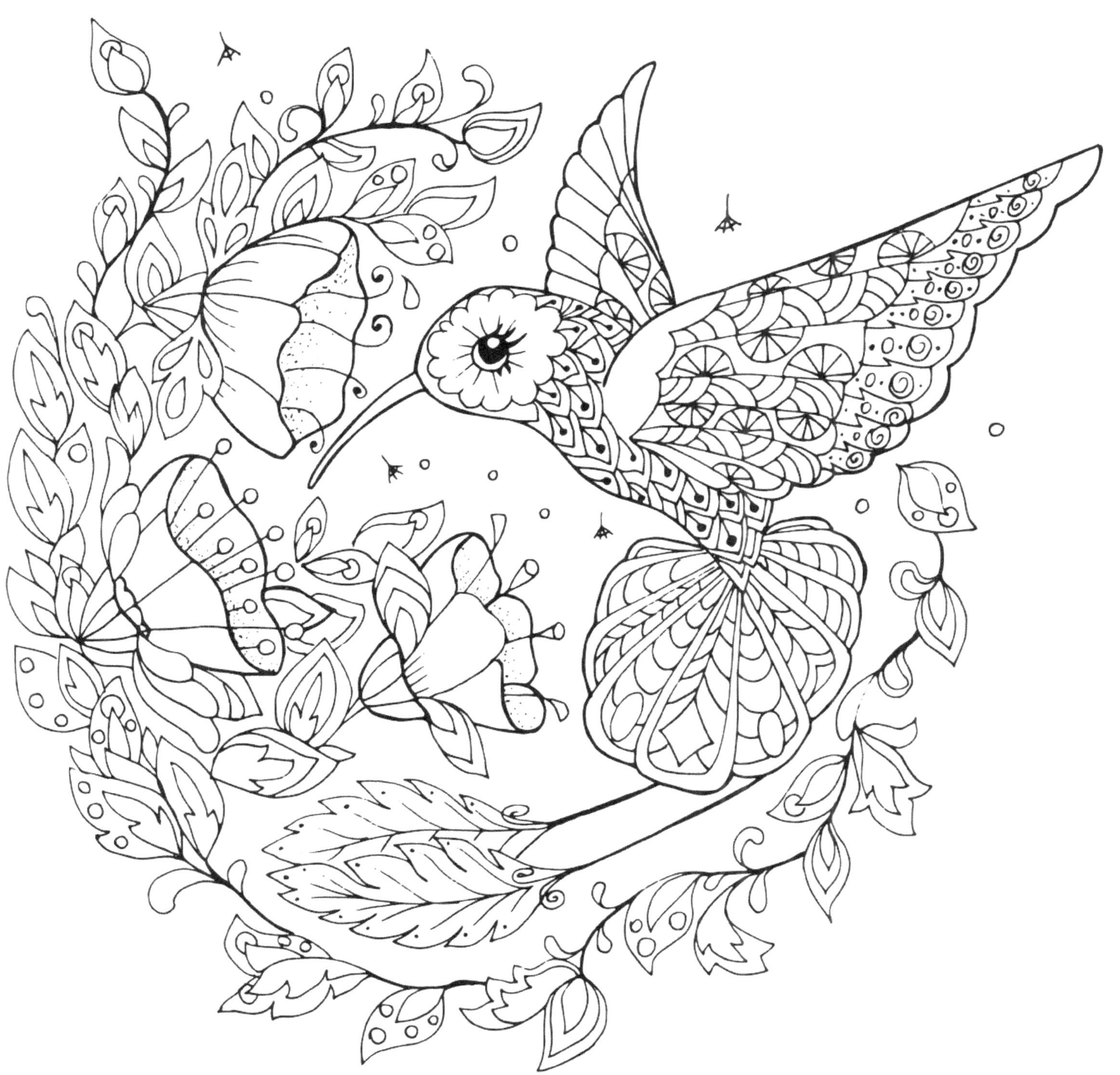

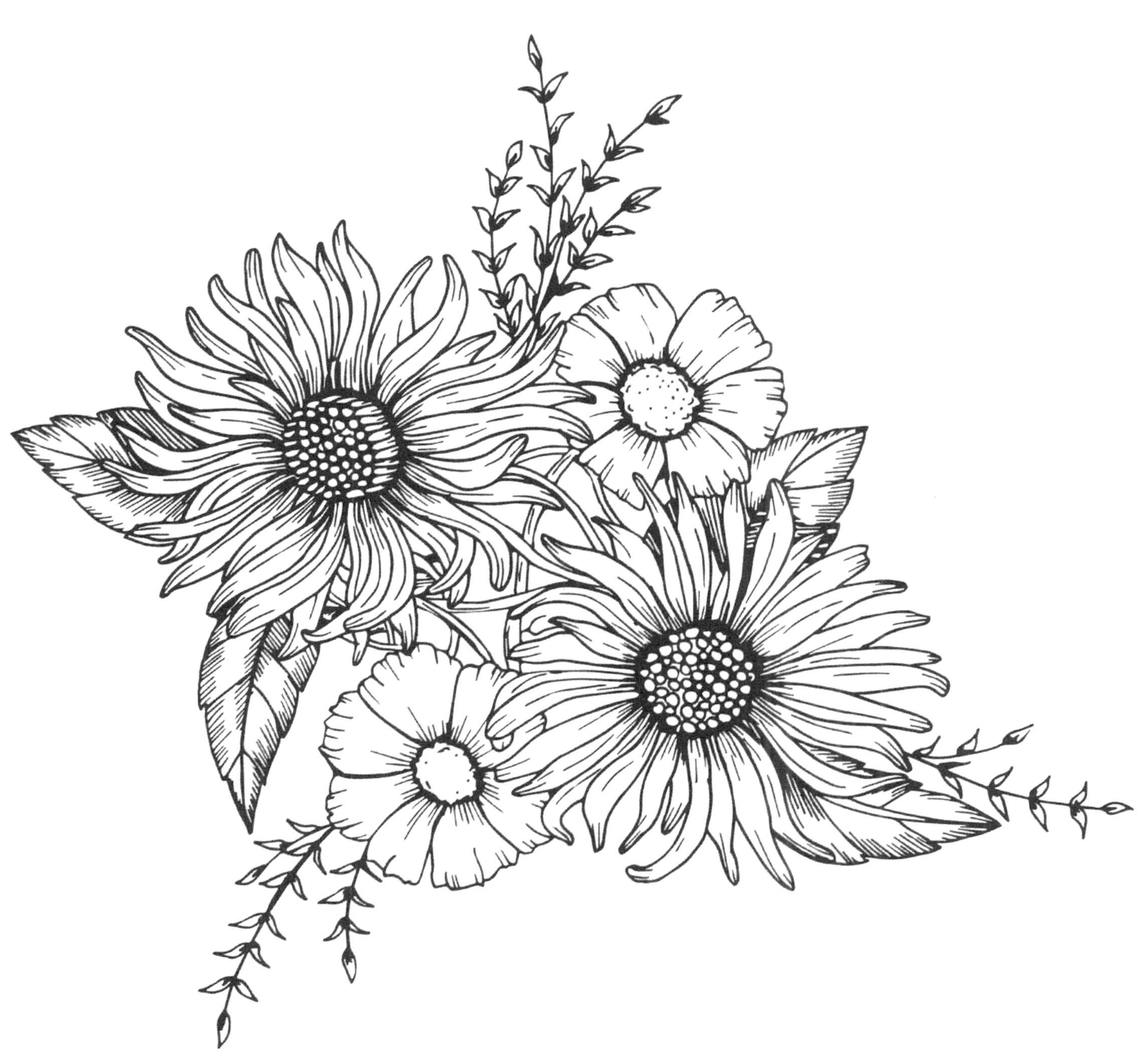

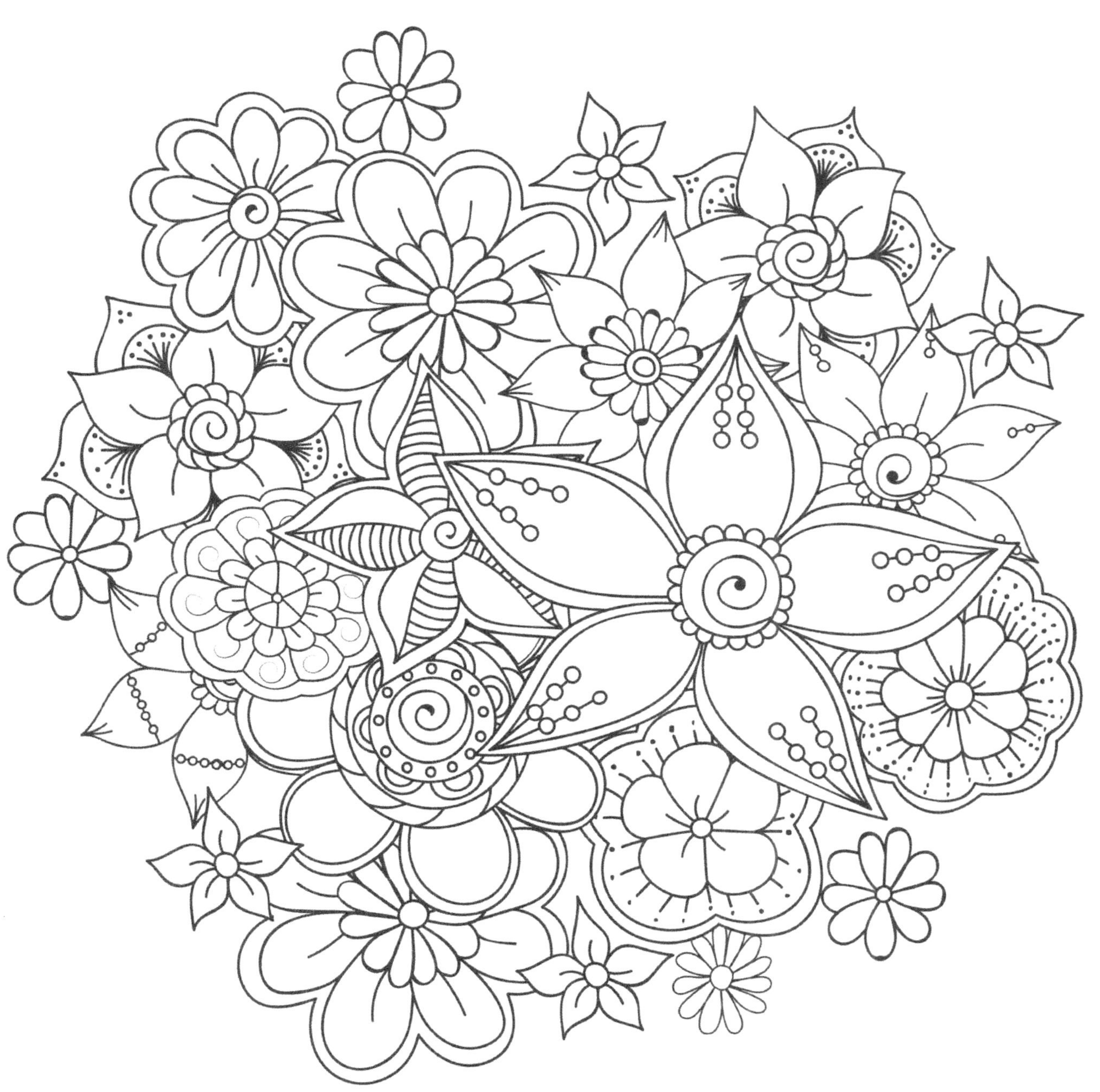

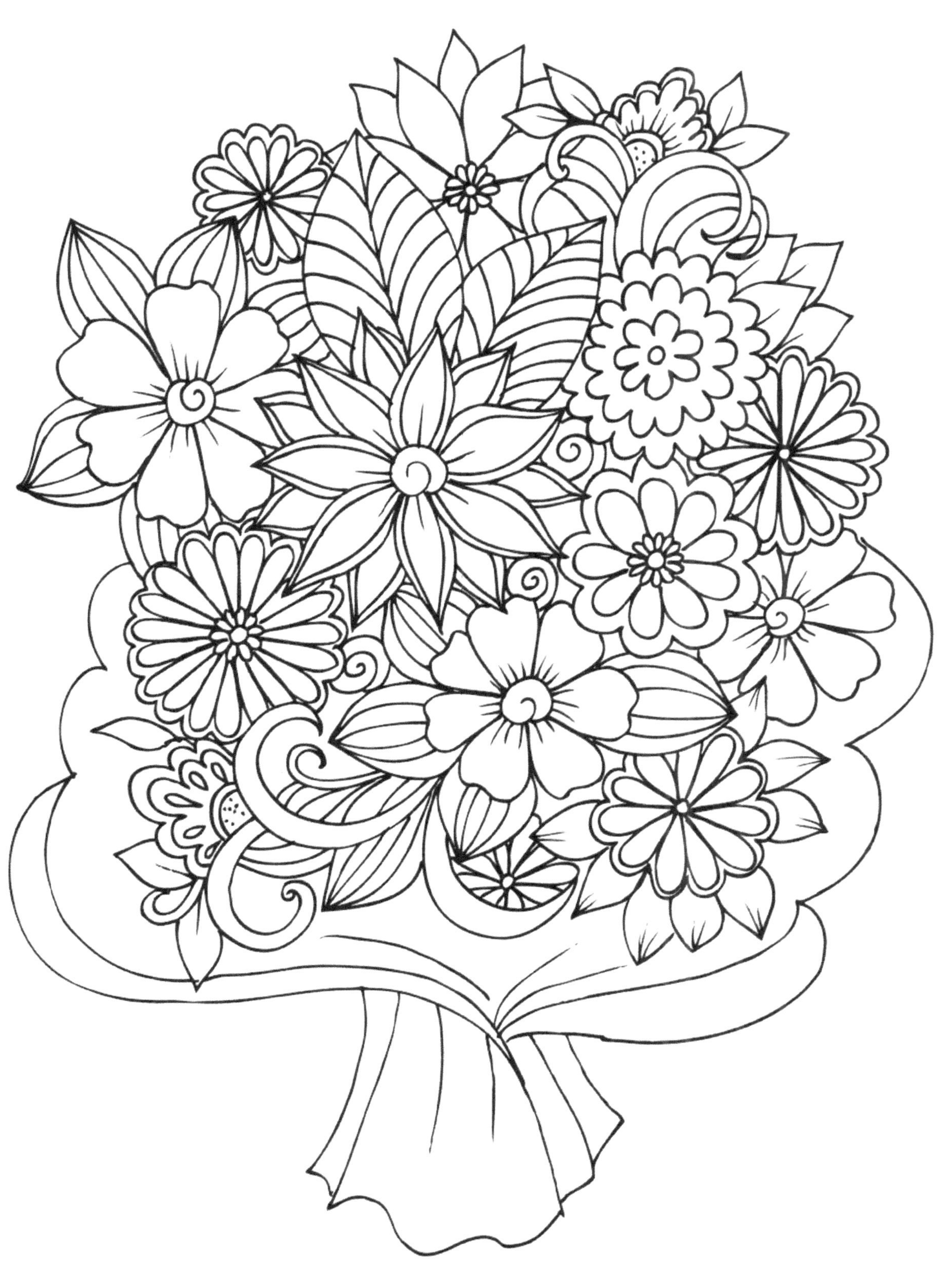

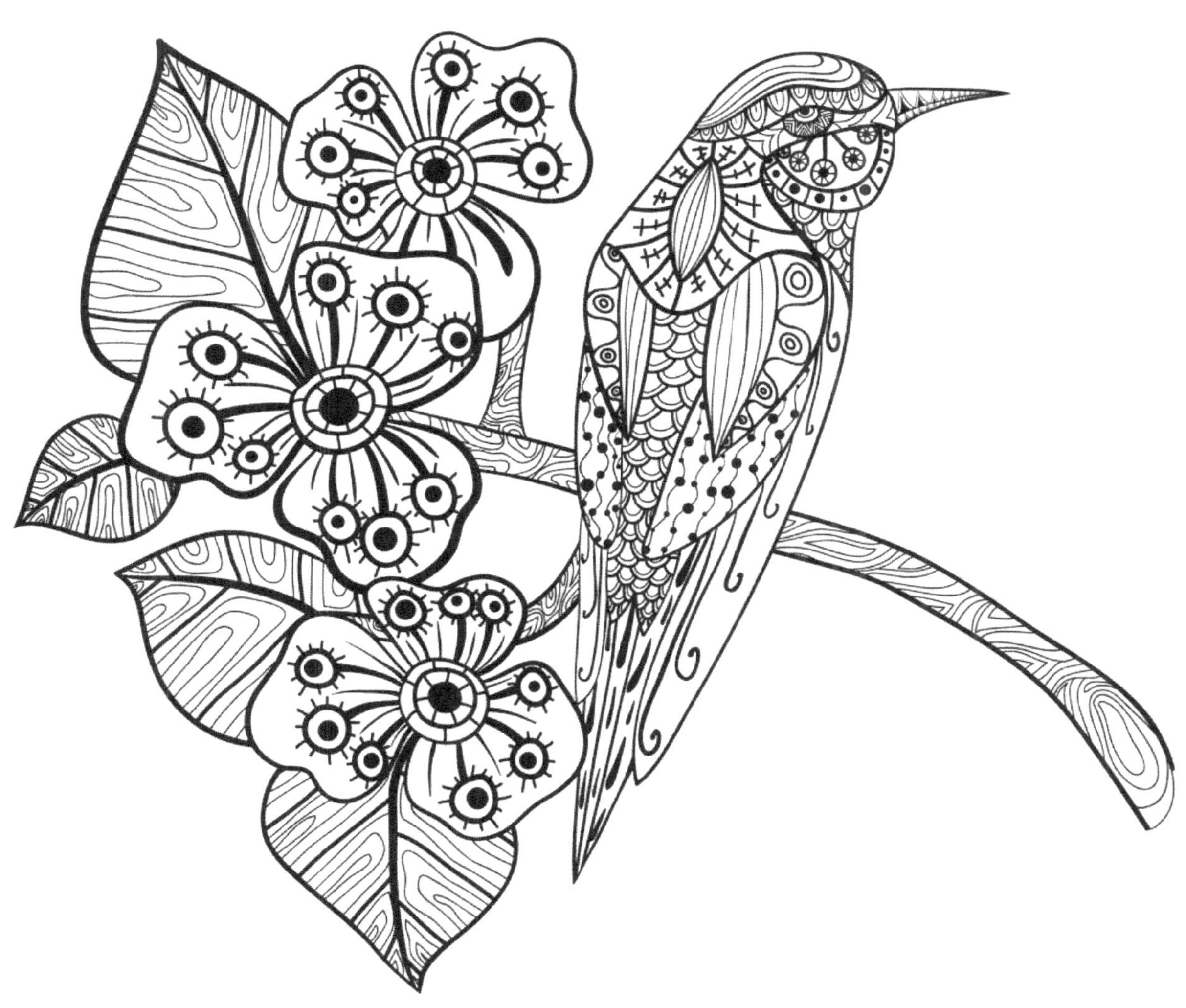

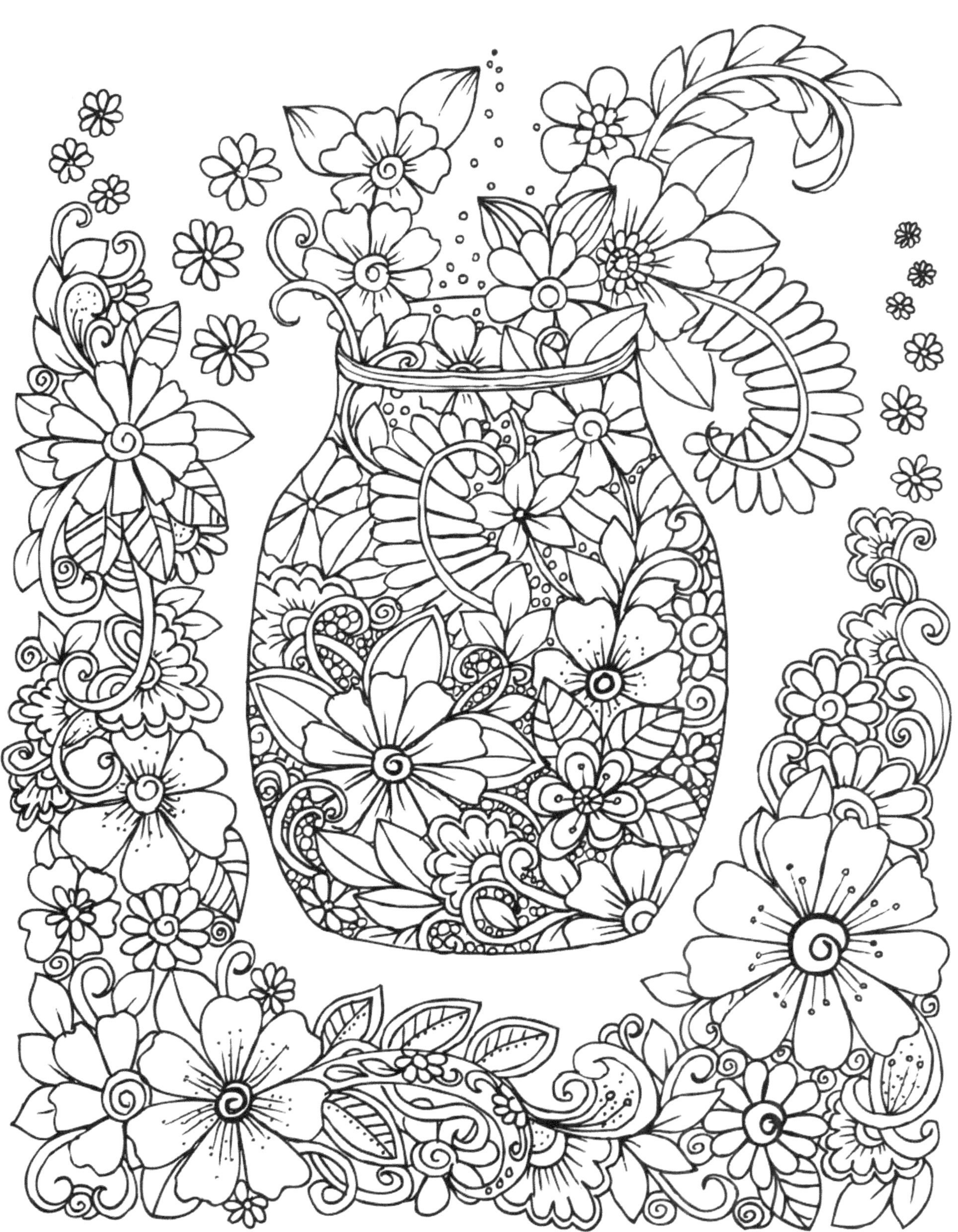

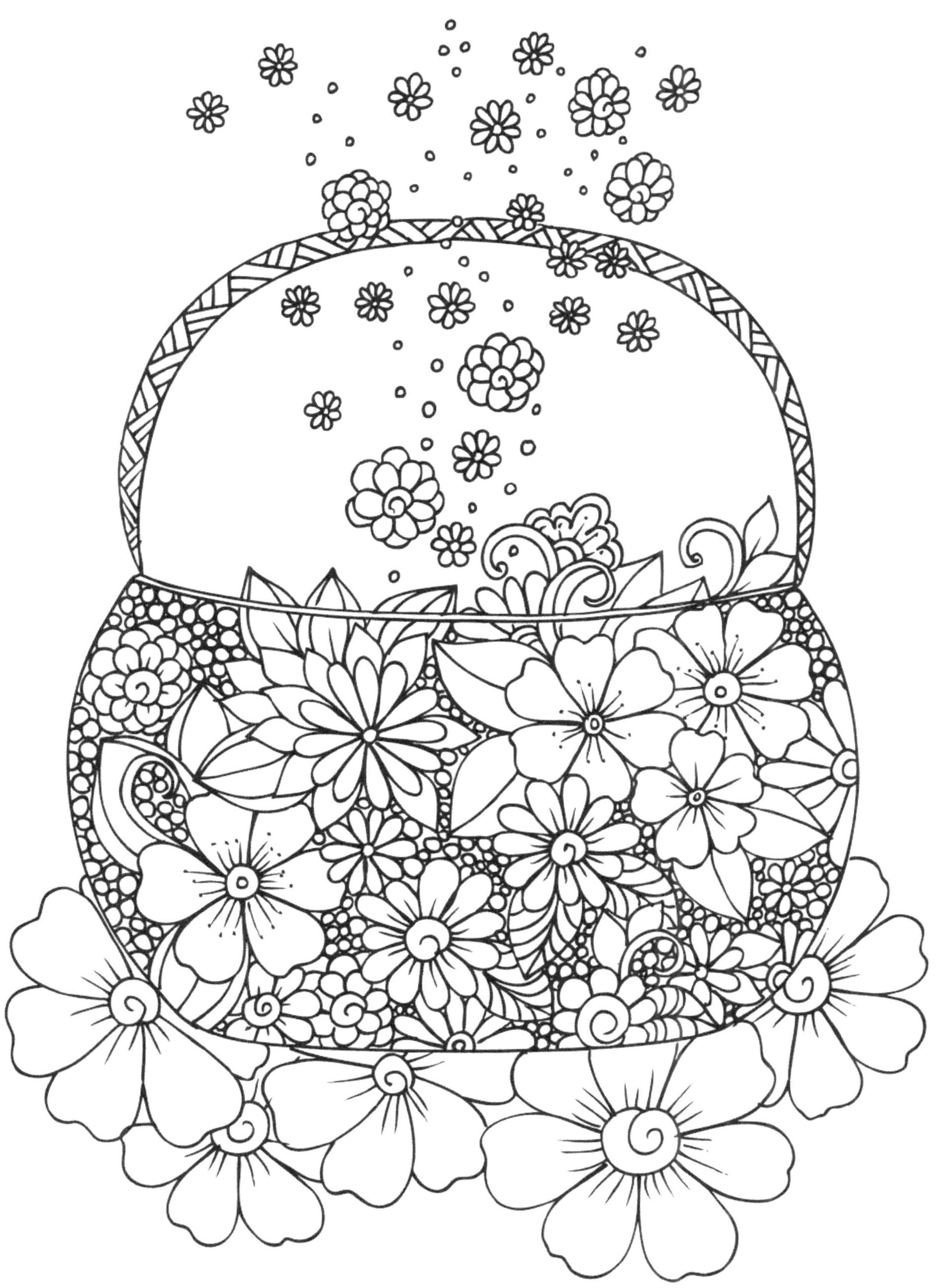

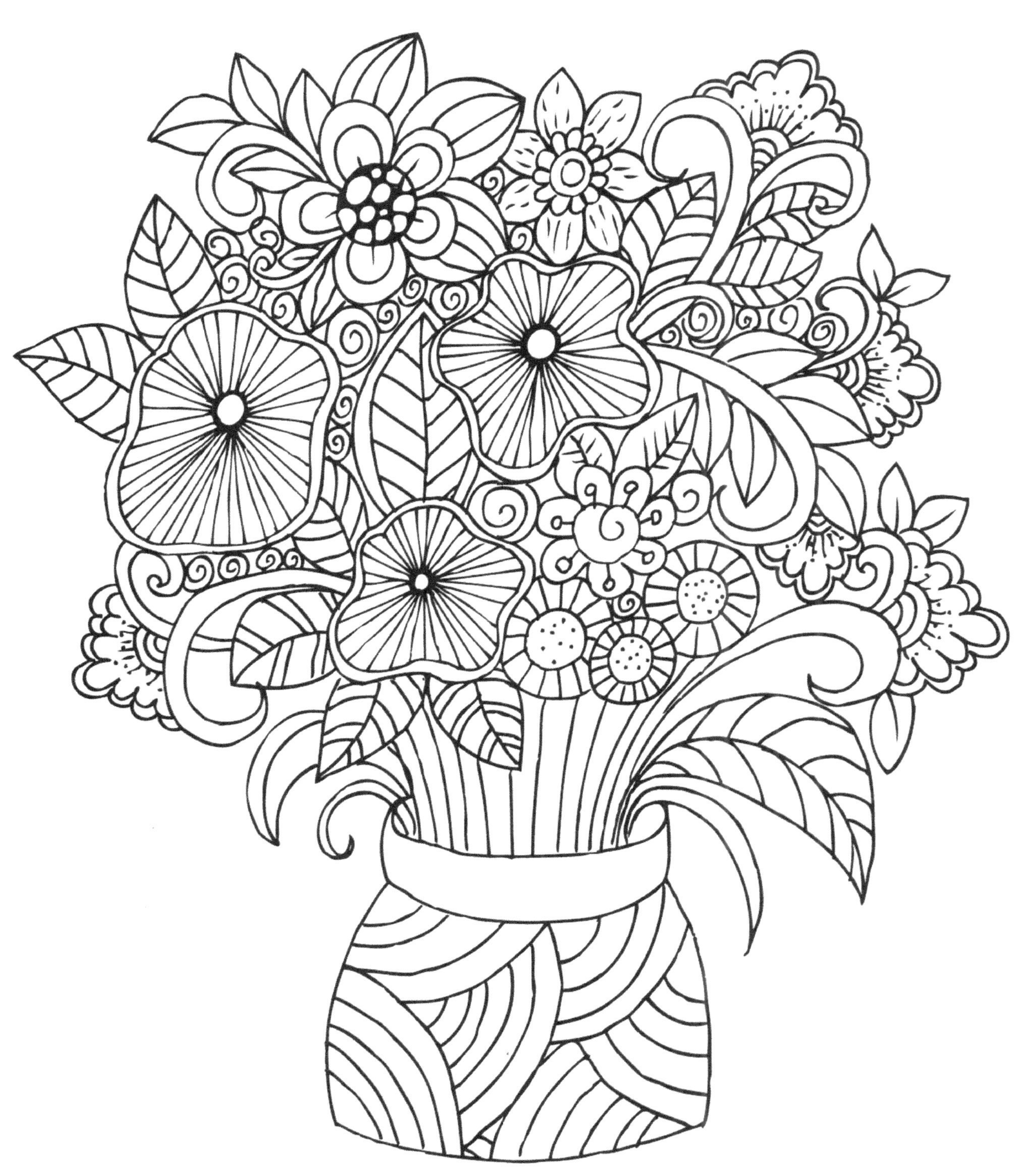

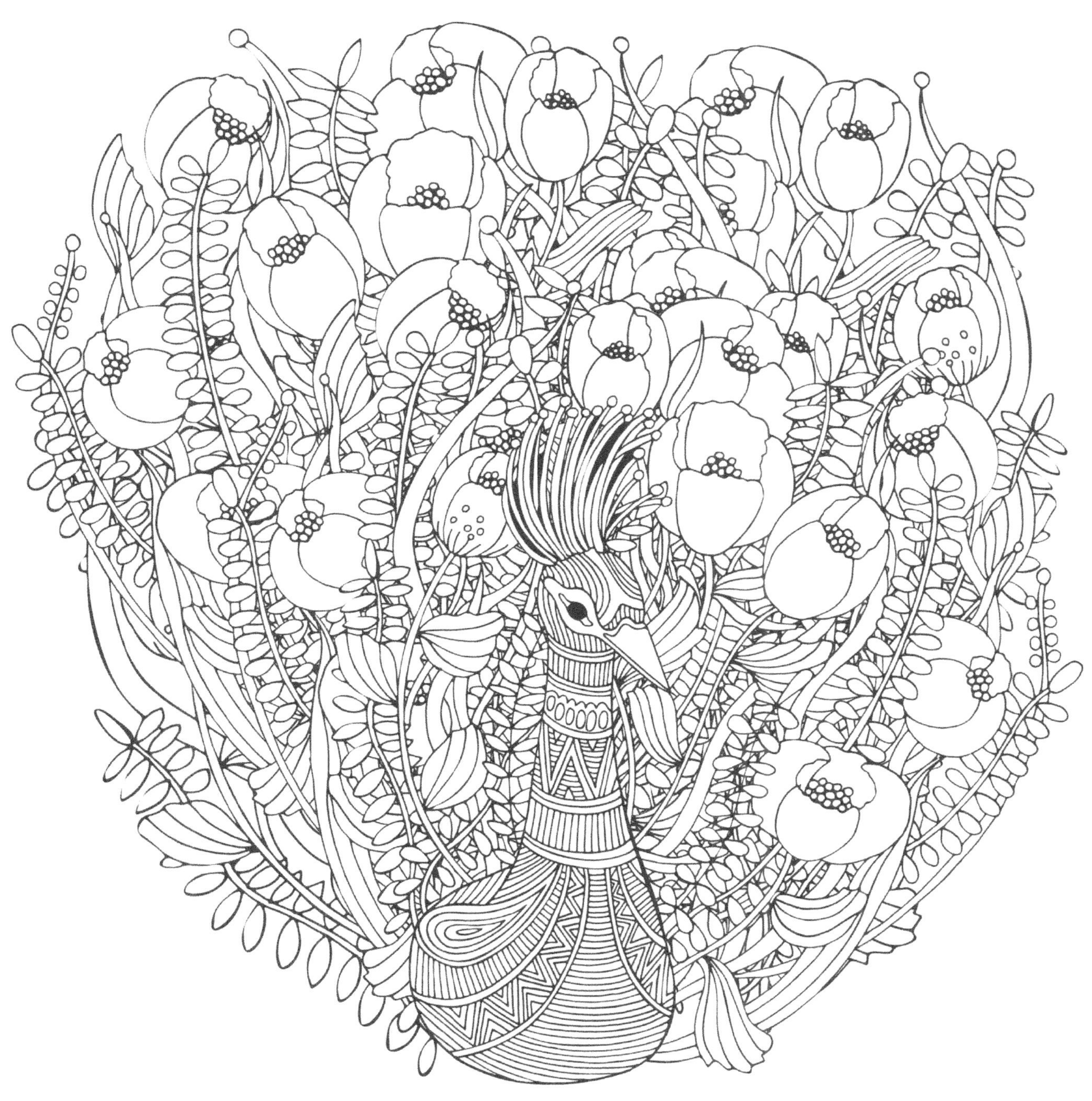

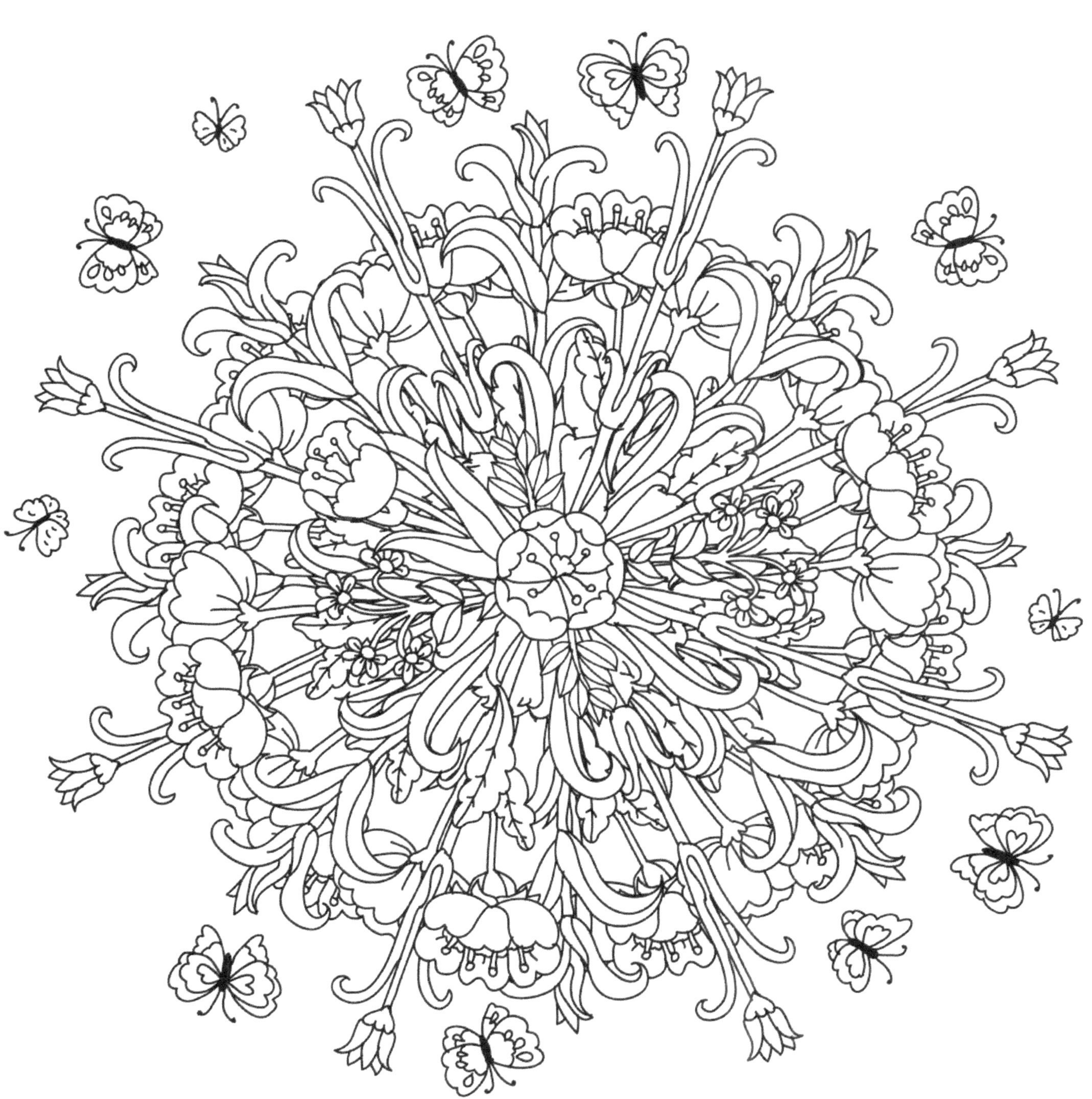

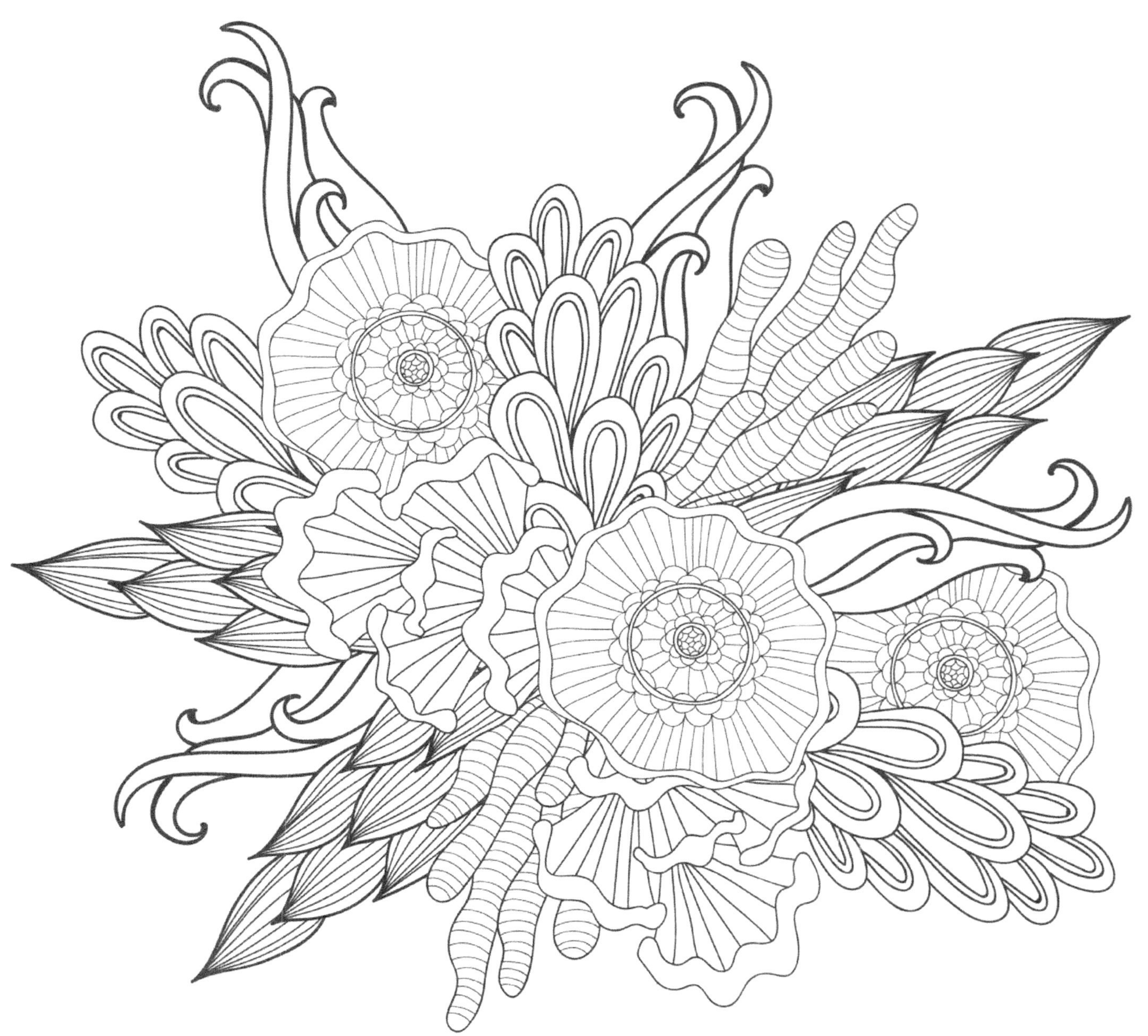

www.ingramcontent.com/pod-product-compliance
Lightning Source LLC
Chambersburg PA
CBHW080401030726
47598CB00010B/2850